CONNOISSEUR'S EDITION

THE HELMSMAN PRESS NEW YORK

AN UNHURRIED VIEW OF EROTICA

WRITTEN BY RALPH GINZBURG WITH AN INTRODUCTION BY DR. THEODOR REIK AND PREFACE BY GEORGE JEAN NATHAN

Library of Congress Catalog Card Number: 58-8260

Designed by Alice Katz

Type Set by The Polyglot Press, New York

Printed and Bound by The Haddon Craftsmen,
Scranton, Pennsylvania

Distributed to retail shops
by Book Sales, Incorporated, New York

Manufactured in the United States of America

Contents

Introduction

At the time when I read newspaper reports of the California libel trial of a magazine that published lurid material about the sex-life of movie stars, my train of thoughts ran to memories of Vienna of my youth. I realized only later on that I must have compared the mental attitude of my native town to sexuality with that of Hollywood because a scene from one of Arthur Schnitzler's plays came to mind. A young man about town encounters a lady of his acquaintanceship: "I have heard many bad things about you, madame," he says. "Let me hope that they are true."

There was as much interest in and gossip about the affairs of heart and plain affairs of celebrities in Vienna as in Hollywood. The satirist Karl Kraus stated that a man taking a walk with a woman on the Ringstrasse was, so to speak, automatically considered her lover. When he was seen walking with a male friend he was considered a homosexual and when he walked alone, the Viennese were convinced that he was a masturbator.

There was enough gossip, mostly allusive and often witty, but there was, of course, no magazine-publicity nor scandal-gathering agency. There was not that lip-smacking, self-conscious and impudent vicarious enjoyment, not that hypocritical moral indignation. There was not that atmosphere of latent puritanism that sees sex as something sinful and rejoices in discovering that other people have sexual functions and desires.

Rumors were not taken with a grain of salt, but of sugar and sexual matters were treated casually, if not jokingly. The Viennese shared the conviction of old, wise Anatole France who then wrote that of all sexual aberrations chastity is the strangest.

This little book deals with the universal interest the Anglo-Saxons had and have in all aspects of sex in a surprising manner. It shows the powerful undercurrent of pornography that runs faithfully with the great stream of literature. It follows the erotic trend that moves under the surface of literature from its beginning of the Anglo-Saxon *Exeter Book* until the pornographic works of our time. The author will readily admit that his book about the erotica in England and America is fragmentary and incomplete, but who can register all the waves of that unending stream?

It is certainly unnecessary in this age of psychoanalysis to state that this book has great scientific value. It shows which components of sexuality and which disavowed impulses strive for satisfaction and which appeal to the appetite of the average man (and woman) of America and England. The excerpts from erotic literature and the data here collected present valuable contributions not only to sexology, but also to the exploration of the life of unconscious emotions. The material here presented will be of great interest to the psychologist and psychiatrist, to the sociologist and historian of civilization and last, but not least, to the connoisseur of literature. Also the bibliophile will find many data, unknown to all, about publications and collections of erotica.

The attentive and thoughtful reader of this book will find that it touches serious problems between its lines, problems intimately connected with the situation of our civilization. If erotica exercises such a passionate spell and awakens such general interest, can we still say "ugly as sin"? It seems sin is very attractive to most, if not to all of us. If it were as repulsive and ugly as they say, why should so many and forceful prohibitions be necessary?

The author justifiably includes the scatological interest in the area of erotica. The discoveries of psychoanalysis and of analytic child-psychology leave no doubt that the functions of evacuation are not only biologically but also psychologically intimately connected with those of sexuality. Yes, in early childhood they cannot be differentiated. Also in the neuroses and psychoses they can replace those of genital trends.

John Wesley's saying that cleanliness is next to godliness becomes very debatable when we find that dirt often functions as excellent protection of virtue that is endangered. Freud told us, his Viennese circle, a telling epigram of Brouardet whose lectures he attended in 1885 when he was a student of Charcot in Paris. Brouardet demonstrated at the Morgue on corpses many parts of neglected evidence, interesting to the physician. He discussed the clues by which one could conjecture the social position and character of unknown persons found dead. Freud heard him once say: "Les genoux sales sont les signes d'une fille honnête." Dirty knees are characteristics of a "nice" girl! Should cleanliness thus be more akin to vice than to virtue? No doubt, the godliness of some saints smelled to high heaven.

We welcome this courageous book that presents a valuable piece of conscientious research.

THEODOR REIK

New York, September, 1957

Preface

My friend Ralph Ginzburg has a mind alert to all the various idiosyncrasies of censorship and knows the different imbecile turns it has periodically taken. There are some shrewd pictures of the censorship mind psychologically illustrated by some strange delvings into the muddy waters of the Ganges. His book, I think, will go a long way to analyze and purify censorship of its muddy stink. It should add a valuable dose of history to the disgraceful general picture of the Bluenose as it has poked into and disturbed the American scene.

GEORGE JEAN NATHAN

New York, January, 1958

Foreword

The late Theodore Schroeder, one of the most obscure but exciting intellectual pioneers in American history, was first to point out the parallel between the "twin superstitions" of witchery and obscenity. Nine million "witches" were tortured to death from the 15th through the 19th centuries, according to best available statistics. Likewise, scores of thousands of writers, bookmen and bibliophiles have been imprisoned and fined for the equally indefinable "crime" of obscenity. Mankind now turns away in shame from the graves of the nine million confirmed "witches" it murdered. And I predict that in one hundred years from now people will look back with equal shame—indeed, if not with side-splitting laughter—at our own recent history wherein the greatest courts of our land and our mightiest police agencies have preoccupied themselves with obscenity as a punishable offense.

As with witchery, no scientific proof has ever been offered to demonstrate the alleged injury which obscenity has wrought. Nor has the "crime" ever been satisfactorily defined.

I bring all this up in connection with my book on erotic literature because of the great number of erotic masterworks which have been thought to be "obscene" in times past.

In this book, I have woven choice samples of English erotic literature into an interpretive and explanatory context. *An Unhurried View Of Erotica* is not an anthology. Anthologies lack the kind of running explanation that is necessary to tie together the elements that make them up. I hope the arrangement of this book will make the erotic samples interesting not only in themselves, but interesting as a group, giving the reader a larger, more meaningful view of the field. Hopefully, in this book the whole will be greater than the sum of its parts.

I would like to express my deep gratitude to the many bibliophiles and professional bookmen and friends who helped me with the tricky job of researching this book. In particular, I am indebted to the staffs of the Library of Congress, the New York Public Library, the New York Academy of Medicine Library, the Armed Forces Medical Library, the Bibliotheque Nationale and the Reading Room of the British Museum.

RALPH GINZBURG

January, 1958

An Unhurried View of Erotica

TO THE FURTHER LIBERATION
OF MAN'S HEALTHIER
INSTINCTS

PART I *Precursors of English Erotica*

GENTLEMEN: with works of erotica, as with the women whose place they are often called upon to take, there are dowdy undistinguished specimens which abound in profusion and there are the rarissimi rarissorum for whose charms men all through the ages have paid dearly both in terms of material and spirit.

This treatise concerns itself with the latter. It does not trifle with variations of a theme as photographed in a Mexican brothel, with specialty playing cards, with binoculars that reveal sultry tableaux when held up to the light, or with twelve-page hip-pocket-size sequences of crudely drawn cartoons which circulate under titles like *Confessions of a Greenwich Village Sofa; The Rover Boys at Radcliffe; Dolly the Itinerant Chambermaid at the New Beverly Hilton;* and *The Exodus of King Farouk, or* [subtitle] *One More for the Road.*

Rather, this treatise is concerned with the hard core of some 2,000 titles of classical erotica in the English language. They are the works which repose today in the Rare Book Rooms and on Restricted Shelves of the world's dozen-or-so leading libraries, books which have somehow survived centuries of prosecution, burning, bowdlerizing, mutilation, concealment, and defenestration to become invaluable artefacts of sexual folklore for men of science and belles-lettres. In short, this book is about the 2,000-odd books that would undoubtedly rank among the all-time best-sellers of the English language if only the public knew more about them and could get their hands on them.

Before we proceed further, however, it is important to state here that the word "erotic" is used in this treatise with its broadest possible meaning, that given by *Webster's Collegiate Dictionary*: "Of, relating to, or treating of sexual love." This is, admittedly, an excessively broad definition. But no truly satisfactory definition of erotica (and/or pornography or obscenity) has ever been devised. The concept is entirely too subjective. As D. H. Lawrence has said, "What is pornography to one man is the laughter of genius to another."

Moreover, sources of sexual stimulation vary not only from man to man, but from culture to culture and from epoch to epoch as well. A cultured Chinese gentleman, for example, once remarked that he found the pulsating rhythms of the U.S. Marine Band uncomfortably stimulating. And Sir Richard Burton tells of the Moslem dignitary who wasn't the least bit perturbed when his wife fell off her camel, inadvertantly revealing her underparts to a large company of Englishmen, for hadn't she kept her face covered throughout the mishap? Nor must we forget that fig leaves on most Greek and Renaissance statues were not appended until the latter days of the Reformation and of Victoria.

Despite these differences in criteria of sexual propriety, however, one thing is clear: eroticism has existed in the arts and letters of almost every civilization in recorded history. Ancient Peruvians took great pride in depicting fantastic coital variations on their ithyphallic pottery. In China, the lubrical novel *Chin P'ing Mei* has been enjoyed for centuries, though until 1912 readers of it risked the penalty of a 100-lash flogging.

In Greek and Roman cultures the role of the erotica was even less abashed. Thus in Sparta the populace was rallied to feasts and the like with erotic songs and jests, and Greek drama, which was related to Greek religion, was frequently erotic in nature. Aristophanes' *Lysistrata* is perhaps our best-known surviving example.

To be sure, the omnipresence of erotica in the lives of the ancients did not lack for its counterpart in vice-suppressors and anti-eroticists. There is record in 378 B.C., for example, of Plato having insisted that the *Odyssey* be expurgated for reading by the juveniles of his day. (This was at least two millenia, it must be remembered, before Estes Kefauver cried out with similar outrage before the citizens of his country.)

Of Roman erotica, much tangible evidence remains. Visitors to the ruins of Pompeii have seen the mosaics depicting the various positions of sexual congress which adorned their ancient boudoirs. More significantly, we have inherited from Rome Ovid's *The Art of Love,* a work which merits some examination here because it introduced the world of Gallantry into literature. There had been nothing like *The Art of Love* in Rome before Ovid's time. *The Art of Love* was first to set the stage for Gallantry in literature, a stage on which English eroticists like the Rochesters, the Buckinghams and many others were later to perform. It was *The Art of Love* which introduced the familiar ingredients of the promenades, the whispered confidences, the secret assignations, the fops and the dandies, the billets-doux, the lover's pleadings, the kissings and the quarrellings, the cuckold husband, the perfume, the courtliness, the wit, the raillery, and the other stock-in-trade elements which were to appear in the centuries of erotic comedy in all languages—including English—that followed.

The Art of Love is a matter-of-fact manual for the hedonistic enjoyment of a woman's body. It is divided into three parts. The first part deals with choosing a woman and is addressed to the male reader. The second part tells how to retain her and is likewise for the men. The third part is addressed to women, with intimate instructions on how best to minister to a man's desires.

The "offensiveness" of this latter part of *The Art of Love* was responsible for Ovid's permanent expulsion from Rome by Emperor Augustus in the year 7 A.D., and the following passage comprises the conclusion of this third part:

"Let every woman learn to know herself, and to enter upon love's battle in the pose best suited to her charms. If a woman has a lovely face, let her lie upon her back, if she prides herself upon her hips let her display them to the best advantage. Melanion bore Atalanta's legs upon his shoulders; if your legs are as beautiful as hers, put them in the same position. If you are short, let your lover be the steed. Andromache, who was as tall as an Amazon, never comported herself like that with Hector. A woman, who is conspicuously tall, should kneel with her head turned slightly sideways. If your thighs are still lovely with the charm of youth, if your bosom is without a flaw, lie aslant upon your couch; and think it not a shame to let your hair float unbraided about your shoulders. If the labours of Lucina have left their mark upon you, then, like the swift Parthia, turn your back to the fray. Love has a thousand postures; the simplest and the least fatiguing is to lie on your right side.

". . . My dear ones, feel the pleasure in the very marrow of your bones; share it fairly with your lover, say pleasant, naughty things the while. And if Nature has withheld from you the sensation of pleasure, than teach your lips to lie and say you feel it all. Unhappy is the woman who feels no answering thrill. But if you have to pretend, don't betray yourself by over-acting. Let your movements and your eyes combine to deceive us, and, gasping, panting, complete the illusion. Alas that the temple of bliss should have its secrets and mysteries. A woman who, after enjoying the delights of love, asks for payment from her lover, cannot surely but be joking. Don't let the light in your bedroom be too bright; there are many things about a woman that are best seen in the dimness of twilight."

Earlier, in a typical portion of the second part of *The Art of Love,* Ovid had advised the men: "Never speak to a woman about her defects . . . Moreover, there are words you can employ to palliate defects. If a woman's skin is blacker than Illyrian pitch, tell her she's a brunette. If she squints a little, tell her she's like Venus. If she's carroty, tell her she's like Minerva. If she's so skinny you would think she was at death's door, tell her she has a graceful figure. If she's short, so much the better, she's all the lighter. If she's thick-waisted, why she's just agreeably plump. Similarly, you must disguise every defect under the name of its nearest quality. Never ask her how old she is, or who was consul when she was born. Leave it to the Censor to perform that uncomfortable duty, especially if she has passed the flower of her youth, if the summer of her days is over, and if she is already compelled to pull out her gray hairs.

". . . Nor should it be forgotten that women, who are getting on in years, have experience . . . They know all the different attitudes of Love and will assume them at your pleasure. No pictured representation can rival them in voluptuousness. With them pleasure comes naturally, without provocation, the pleasure which is sweeter than all, the pleasure which is shared equally by the man and the woman. I hate those embraces in which both do not consummate; that is why boys please me but little. I hate a woman who offers herself because she ought to do so, and, cold and dry, thinks of her sewing when she's making love. The pleasure that is granted to me from a sense of duty ceases to be a pleasure at all. I won't have any woman doing her duty towards me. How sweet it is to hear her voice quaver as she tells me the joy she feels, and hear her imploring me to slacken my speed so as to prolong her bliss. How I love to see her drunk with delight, gazing with swooning eyes upon me, or, languishing with love, keeping me a long while at arms' length. . . .

"If you listen to my advice, you will not be in too great a hurry to attain the limits of your pleasure. Learn, by skilful dallying, to reach the goal by gentle, pleasant stages. When you have found the sanctuary of bliss, let no foolish modesty arrest your hand. Then will you see the love-light trembling in her eyes, even as the rays of the sun sparkle on the dancing waves. Then will follow gentle moanings mingled with murmurings of love, soft groans and sighs and whispered words that sting and lash desire. But now beware! Take heed lest, cramming on too much sail, you speed too swiftly for your mistress. Now should you suffer her to outstrip you. Speed on together towards the promised haven. The height of bliss is reached when, unable any longer to withstand the wave of pleasure, lover and mistress at one and the same moment are overcome. Such should be thy rule when time is yours and fear does not compel you to hasten your stolen pleasures. Nevertheless, if there be danger in delay, lean well forward, and drive your spur deep into your courser's side.

"My task draws toward its end. Young lovers, show your gratitude. Lovers, laud your poet, sing my praises, so that my name may resound throughout the world."

In the English language, erotica is just about as old as the language itself. First traces are seen in the gross riddles of the Anglo-Saxon *Exeter Book,* a work lovingly compiled as a labor of piety by a monk in that day before bawdry was considered to be indecent. We also see it in the first great poem of the English language, Chaucer's *Canterbury Tales,* wherein the Wife of Bath gleefully proclaims the insatiability of her venereal cravings. And we see it again all through the Golden Age of Elizabeth when English letters witnessed its greatest genius.

But erotica then was not yet the tendentious sensuality that we have since become accustomed to. It was naive rather than studied, jocular rather than intent. Always there was the gag-ending, the punch-line, as in *A Cure For The Plague* which tells the story of three male volunteers who lay with a maiden afflicted with the plague. In administering their own private prescriptions for her illness to the maiden while she is in bed, all three volunteers die, of course, and the maiden survives.

The following is a typical fifteenth century erotic story. It comes from a book which appeared originally in French under title of *Les Cent Nouvelles Nouvelles.* Authorship of the book has often been attributed to Prince Louis XI, later King of France. Title of the book in English is *One Hundred Merrie And Delightsome Stories . . . Right Pleasaunt To Relate In All Goodly Companie By Way Of Joyance And Jollity.* In 1899 a superb edition of this book was issued in English from the secret press of Charles Carrington in Monmartre, Paris, together with a set of fifty-two original, full page colored engravings. This is the first story in the book and is titled *The Reverse of the Medal:*

"In the town of Valenciennes there lived formerly a notable citizen, who had been receiver of Hainault, who was renowned amongst all others for his prudence and discretion, and amongst his praiseworthy virtues, liberality was not the least, and thus it came to pass that he enjoyed the grace of princes, lords, and other persons of good estate. And this happy condition, Fortune granted and preserved him to the end of his days.

"Both before and after death unloosed him from the chains of matrimony, the good citizen mentioned in this story, was not so badly lodged in the said town but that many a great lord would have been content and honoured to have such a lodging. His house faced several streets, in one of which was a little postern door, opposite to which lived a good comrade of his, who had a pretty wife, still young and charming.

"And as is customary, her eyes, the archers of the heart, shot so many arrows into the said citizen, that unless he found some present remedy, he felt his case was no less than mortal.

"To more surely prevent such a fate, he found many and subtle manners of making the good comrade, the husband of the said quean, his private and familiar friend, so that few of the dinners, suppers, banquets, baths, and other amusements took place, either in the hotel or elsewhere, without his company. And of such favours his comrade was very proud, and also happy.

"When our citizen, who was more cunning than a fox, had gained the good-will of his friend, little was needed to win the love of his wife, and in a few days he had worked so much and so well that the gallant lady was fain to hear his case, and to provide a suitable remedy thereto. It remained but to provide time and place; and for this she promised him that, whenever her husband lay abroad for a night, she would advise him thereof.

"The wished-for day arrived when the husband told his wife that he was going to a chateau some three leagues distant from Valenciennes, and charged her to look after the house and keep within doors, because his business would not permit him to return that night.

"It need not be asked if she was joyful, though she showed it not either in word, or deed, or otherwise. Her husband had not journeyed a league before the citizen knew that the opportunity had come.

"He caused the baths to be brought forth, and the stoves to be heated, and pasties, tarts, and hippocras, and all the rest of God's good gifts, to be prepared largely and magnificently.

"When evening came, the postern door was unlocked, and she who was expected entered thereby, and she was kindly received.

"Then they ascended into a chamber, and washed in a bath, by the side of which a good supper was quickly laid and served. They drank often and deeply. To speak of the wines and viands would be a waste of time and, to cut the story short, there was plenty of everything. In this most happy condition passed the great part of this sweet but short night; kisses often given and often returned, until they desired nothing but to go to bed.

"Whilst they were thus making good cheer, the husband returned from his journey, and knowing nothing of this adventure, knocked loudly at the door of the house. And the company that was in the antechamber refused him entrance until he should name his surety.

"Then he gave his name loud and clear, and so his good wife and the citizen heard him and knew him. She was so amazed to hear the voice of her husband that her loyal heart almost failed her; and she would have fainted, had not the good citizen and his servants comforted her.

"The good citizen being calm and well advised how to act, made haste to put her to bed, and lay close by her; and charged her well that she should lie close to him and hide her face, so that no one could see it. And that being done as quickly as may be, yet without too much haste, he ordered that the door should be opened. Then his good comrade sprang into the room, thinking to himself that there must be some mystery, else they had not kept him out of the room. And when he saw the table laid with wines and goodly viands, also the bath finely prepared, and the citizen in a handsome bed, well curtained, with a second person by his side, he spoke loudly, and praised the good cheer of his neighbour. He called him rascal, and whoremonger, and drunkard, and many other names, which made those who were in the chamber laugh long and loud; but his wife could not join in the mirth, her face being pressed to the side of her new friend.

"'Ha!' said the husband, 'Master whore-monger, you have well hidden from me this good cheer; but, by my faith, though I was not at the feast, you must show me the bride.'

"And with that, holding a candle in his hand, he

drew near the bed, and would have withdrawn the coverlet, under which, in fear and silence, lay his most good and perfect wife; when the citizen and his servants prevented him; but he was not content, and would by force, in spite of them all, have laid his hand upon the bed.

"But he was not master there, and could not have his will, and for good cause, and was fain to be content with a most gracious proposal which was made to him, and which was this, that he should be shown the backside of his wife, and her haunches, and thighs—which were big and white, and moreover fair and comely—without uncovering and beholding her face.

"The good comrade, still holding a candle in his hand, gazed for long without saying a word; and when he did speak, it was to praise highly the great beauty of that dame, and he swore by a great oath that he had never seen anything that so much resembled the back parts of his own wife, and that were he not well sure that she was at home at that time, he would have said it was she.

"She had by this somewhat recovered, and he drew back much disconcerted, but they all told him, first one and then the other, that he had judged wrongly, and spoken against the honour of his wife, and that this was some other woman, as he would afterwards see for himself.

"To restore him to good humour, after they had thus paused his eyes, the citizen ordered that they should make him sit at the table, where he drowned his suspicions by eating and drinking of what was left of the supper, whilst they in the bed were robbing him of his honour.

"The time came to leave, and he said good night to the citizen and his companions, and begged they would let him leave by the postern door, that he might the sooner return home. But the citizen replied that he knew not then where to find the key; he thought also that the lock was so rusted that they could not open the door, which they rarely if ever used. He was content therefore to leave by the front gate, and make a long detour to reach his house, and whilst the servants of the citizen led him to the door, the good wife was quickly on her feet, and in a short time, clad in a simple sark with her corset on her arm, and come to the postern. She made but one bound to her house, where she awaited her husband (who came by a longer way) well prepared as to the manner in which she should receive him.

"Soon came our man, and seeing still a light in the house, knocked at the door loudly; and this good wife, who was pretending to clean the house, and had a besom in her hands, asked—what she knew well; 'Who is there?'

"And he replied; 'It is your husband.'

"'My husband!' said she. 'My husband is not here! He is not in the town!'

"With that he knocked again, and cried, 'Open the door! I am your husband.'

"'I know my husband well,' quoth she, 'and it is not his custom to return home so late at night, when he is in the town. Go away, and do not knock here at this hour.'

"But he knocked all the more, and called her by name once or twice. Yet she pretended not to know him, and asked why he came at that hour, but for all reply he said nothing but, 'Open! Open!'

"'Open!' said she. 'What! are you still there you rascally whore-monger? By St. Mary, I would rather see you drown than come in here! Go! and sleep as badly as you please in the place where you came from.'

"Then her good husband grew angry, and thundered against the door as though he would knock the house down, and threatened to beat his wife, such was his rage,—of which she had not great fear; but at length, because of the noise be made, and that she might the better speak her mind to him, she opened the door, and when he entered, he saw an angry face, and had a warm greeting. For when her tongue found words from a heart overcharged with anger and indignation, her language was sharp as well-ground Guingant razors.

"And, amongst other things, she reproached him that he had wickedly pretended a journey in order that he might try her, and that he was a coward and a recreant, unworthy to have such a wife as she was.

"Our good comrade, though he had been angry, saw how wrong he had been, and restrained his wrath, and the indignation that in his heart he had conceived when he was standing outside the door was turned aside. So he said, to excuse himself, and to satisfy his wife, that he had returned from his journey because he had forgotten a letter concerning the object of his going.

"Pretending not to believe him, she invented more stories, and charged him with having frequented taverns and bagnios, and other improper and dissolute resorts, and that he behaved as no respectable man should, and she cursed the hour in which she had made his acquaintance, and doubly cursed the day she became his wife.

"The poor man, much grieved, seeing his wife more troubled than he liked, knew not what to say. And his suspicions being removed, he drew near her, weeping and falling upon his knees and made the following fine speech:

"'My most dear companion, and most loyal wife, I beg and pray of you to remove from your heart the wrath you have conceived against me, and pardon me for all that I have done against you. I own my fault, I see my error. I have come now from a place where they made good cheer, and where, I am ashamed to say, I fancied I recognized you, at which I was much displeased. And so I wrongfully and causelessly suspected you to be other than a good woman, of which I now repent bitterly, and pray of you to forgive me, and pardon my folly.'

"The good woman, seeing her husband so contrite, showed no great anger.

"'What?' said she, 'You have come from filthy houses of ill-fame, and you dare to think that your honest wife would be seen in such places?'

"'No, no, my dear, I know you would not. I beseech you, say no more about it,' said the good man, and repeated his aforesaid request.

"She, seeing his contrition, ceased her reproaches, and little by little regained her composure, and with much ado pardoned him, after he had made a hundred thousand oaths and promises to her who had so wronged him. And from that time forth she often, without fear or regret, passed the said postern, nor were her escapades discovered by him who was most concerned."

French historians aver incidentally, that this tale is based on a true experience of Louis, Duc d'Orleans who was an accomplished seducer of Court ladies. A voluptuous noblewoman was sleeping with him when her husband came into the chamber to wish the Duke good-day. The Duke covered the lady's head with the sheet, and uncovered the rest of her body. He permitted the husband a caress or two, but forbade him, as he valued his life, to uncover her head. The next night the husband, in bed with his wife, told her that the Duke had shown him the most beautiful naked woman he had ever seen, but he could report nothing of her face. Scandal at the time named the lady as Mariette d'Enghien, the mother of the brave and handsome Comte de Dunois, known in French history as "the Bastard of Orleans."

PART II *Earliest English Works*

DESPITE THE presence in the Middle Ages of the light, jocular sex story, genuine, 100%, lip-smacking, cheek-flushing erotica and pornography did not make its appearance until the Restoration period in the latter 17th century. For it was then that Englishmen first turned themselves to a conscious refinement of their manners. The earliest anti-obscenity laws were devised and, with them, English writers found themselves for the first time with an incentive to flaunt their erotic fantasies before the reading public.

Poetry, which has always been the most eloquent medium for love expression, was first to reflect the heightened sensuality of English letters. At the beginning, the tendency was still largely toward daintiness instead of passion. The phrases were flowery, rather than carnal, but then the double-entendre made its appearance, soon to be followed by bald erotic statement.

The ballad, most irreverent, vigorous and highly contemporary of all poetry, clearly shows the pall of "naughtiness" that had suddenly fallen over sex in the 17th century. Here are two examples. The first ballad is by Sir Charles Sedley, a poet of some note. Sir Sedley, a boon companion of Charles II, was a reveler of great repute and in June, 1663, caused a near riot when, inflamed with alcohol, he disrobed on the balcony of a house near Covent Garden and proceeded to shower the crowd below with excrement and derision. His poetry is somewhat less direct than his mien, but perhaps is just as forceful. Here is a sample:

YOUNG CORIDON AND PHILLIS

by Sir Charles Sedley

Young Coridon and Phillis
  Sate in a Lovely Grove;
Contriving Crowns of Lillies,
  Repeating Tales of Love:
And something else, but what I dare not name.

But as they were a Playing,
  She oagled so the Swain;
It sav'd her plainly saying
  Let's kiss to ease our Pain:
And something else, but what I dare not name.

A thousand times he kiss'd her,
  Laying her on the Green;
But as he farther press'd her,
  Her pretty Leg was seen:
And something else, but what I dare not name.

So many Beauties removing,
  His Ardour still increas'd;
And greater Joys pursuing,
  He wander'd o'er her Breast:
And something else, but what I dare not name.

A last Effort she trying,
  His passion to withstand;
Cry'd but it was faintly crying,
  Pray take away your hand:
And something else, but what I dare not name.

Young Coridon grown bolder,
  The Minute would improve;
This is the time he told her,
  To shew you how I love;
And something else, but what I dare not name.

The Nymph seem'd almost dying,
  Dissolv'd in amorous heat;
She kiss'd and told him sighing,
  My dear your Love is great:
And something else, but what I dare not name.

But Phillis did recover
  Much sooner than the Swain;
She blushing ask'd her Lover,
  Shall we not kiss again:
And something else, but what I dare not name.

Thus Love his Revels keeping,
  'Til Nature at a stand;
From talk they fell to Sleeping,
  Holding each others Hand;
And something else, but what I dare not name.

As has been stated, Sir Sedley was a member of Court and a man of some nobility. But the common ballader, the "street balladeer" who earned his bread hawking penny "broadsides" through the towns and hamlets of England, was as quick as the nobility to seize upon the new attitudes toward sex and to make them the subjects of his balladry. The following street ballad comes from the Nottingham University Library Collection of Original Broadsides and demonstrates as clearly as Sedley's poem the allure that the mere suggestiveness of sex had already acquired.

THE WIDOW THAT KEEPS THE COCK INN

A traveller for many long years I have been,
  But I never went over to France—
Most cities and all market towns I've been in,
  From Berwick on Tweed to Penzance,
Many hotels and taverns I've been in my time,
  And many fair landladys seen—

But of all the fair charmers who other outshine
Give me the sweet widow—
The dear little widow,
I mean the sweet widow that keeps the Cock Inn.

Her lips are as roses as e'en is her wine,
And like all her liquors, she's neat,
She's full of good spirits, that's really divine
And while serving her bitters, looks sweet;
Excuse these outpourings, they spring from the heart,
You may laugh—so shall I, if I win,
One smile of consent, how 'twould lessen the smart,
From the active young widow,
The spruce little widow,
little widow that keeps the Cock Inn.

There's Bet at the 'Blossom' and Poll of the 'Crown,'
Fat Dolly who owns the 'Red Heart.'
There's Kate of the 'Garter and Star,' of renown
And Peggy who keeps the 'Skylark.'
Spruce Fan of the 'Eagle' and Nan of the 'Bell'
Pretty Jane of the 'Man drest in Green';
But of all the fair creatures that others excel,
Give me the sweet widow,
The nice little widow,
My neat pretty widow who keeps the Cock Inn.

There's Nance at 'the Old Woman clothed in Gray'
I look black upon her I vow,
Even Letty who graces 'the Old Load of Hay,'
I don't care a straw for her now;
There's another decanter'd just now in my heart
I for none of the rest care a pin.

Oh, that Cupid the rogue, would but let fly his dart,
At the plump little widow,
The gay little widow,
The spirited widow that keeps the Cock Inn.

When last in her little bar parlour I sat
I joked her about her lone state.
A brood of young chicken's dear widow mind that,
Would be better around you prate,
Says she, pray don't reckon 'fore they are hatch'd;
says I, where's the harm or the sin?
You can manage a second, we're very well match'd
You dear little widow,
You charming young widow,
You're a nice little widow to keep the Cock Inn.

Then here's to the dear little charmer I prize,
In a bumper now filled to the brim,
For who could resist such a pair of black eyes,
As in rich liquid moisture they swim;
Away, then away, with my bachelor's vow,
My hand then is hers, with the ring,
For if she be willing to take me in tow,
I'll marry the widow,
The dear little widow,
I'll marry the widow, and keep the Cock Inn.

In prose, erotic works by the dozens began to spew forth almost as quickly as the poetry. They bore such precis-like titles as:

The Trial of Lord Audley for Abetting a Rape Upon His Countess, Committing Sodomy With

His Servants and Commanding and Countenancing the Debauching of His Daughter.

Adultery on the Part of Married Women and Fornication on the Part of Old Maids and Widows, Defended by Mary Wilson, Spinster, With Plans for Promoting Same.

Memoirs and Adventures of a Flea.

Ten Years of the Life of a Courtesan—Detailing Her First Lessons in Lust, Her Seduction and Voluptuous Life, the Piquant Penchants of Her Various Lovers, etc. Illustrated.

Kate Handcock, or a Young Girl's Introduction To a Fast Life.

The Secret History of Betty Ireland, Containing an Account of Her Unfortunate Marriage, Her Turning Prostitute, and Her Incest With Her Own Son.

The Exciting and Voluptuous Pleasures to be Derived from Crushing and Humiliating the Spirit of a Beautiful and Modest Young Lady.

This surging interest of the English-speaking people in full-charged erotic literature was helped along by the Crown's first attempt in 1708 to condemn a book as obscene. *The Fifteen Plagues of a Maidenhead* was the work involved. In the eyes of the court, however, the book proved worthier than the prosecution's case and it wasn't till twenty years later that the Government was able to secure its first obscenity conviction. A pornography publisher named Edmund Curll had turned out a pornographic work titled *Venus in the Cloister, or the Nun in Her Smock,* and for it was sentenced to the pillory at Charing Cross. But so warmly had the public-at-large received the book and so dearly-beloved was the publisher for it, that the *States Trials Record* indicates "He was not pelted or used ill while in the pillory and when he was taken down out of it, the mob carried him off as it were in triumph to a neighboring tavern."

The themes running through this new English erotica were few in number. The deprecation of lese majesté was a favorite, as in *Adventures of a King's Page* wherein a king is cuckolded by a manservant of great amorous capacity. Again, in *The Castrated Clerk,* the wily minion of a London advocate deceives his master into believing he possesses no testicles and is accordingly entrusted with guarding his employer's mistress, whose body he proceeds to enjoy freely.

Another consistent topic was the love lives and alleged mattress gymnastics of contemporary and historical figures, with French personages appearing as an especial favorite. Typical works were *The Confessions of Marie Antoinette, The Love Cabinet of Madame De Pompadour, and Les Amours De Napoleon.* The latter was an English work deliberately titled in French, like many others, because French was thought to be the most "obscene" of all languages because of its countless love words. An early American work, *The Amorous Intrigues of Aaron Burr,* also falls into this "famous celebrities" category, as do the books which later revolved around the notorious life of Lord Byron, books like: *The Secret Loves of Byron, Byron's Intrigues with Celebrated Women,* and *The Connections of Lord Byron with Ladies of Rank and Fame.* By Victoria's day, so many celebrities had become involved in erotic plots that it became almost fashionable for members of the haut monde to find themselves in printed erotic imbroglio and there is evidence that a number of great reputations were deliberately risked to achieve this distinction.

Religion in general and anti-Catholicism in particular were other consistent themes of erotica. The nuns of early Venice, whose parlors witnessed merriment and license little in accordance with their religious vows, provided many a plot, as in some of the following from this anti-religious category:

The Enterprising Friars.

The Abbess Cured, Being An Account of a Novitiate Who Was Ill for Want of—You Know What—But Would not Have It, Fearing to Be Reproached by Her Nuns, Until all Agreed to Do the Same to Keep Her Company and Most Willingly Did so.

The Pope Maker, Being the Delightsome Story of a Hermit Who Deceived the Daughter of a Poor Woman, Making Her Believe that Her Daughter Should Have a Son by Him Who Should Become

Pope and How, When She Brought Forth, It Was a Girl, and Thus Was the Trickery of the Hermit Discovered, and for That Cause He Had to Flee That Country.

Occasionally, eroticists would wander off into the badlands of scatalogia as in *The Benefit of Farting Explained,* "Wrote in Spanish by a Professor of Bumbast in the University of Craccow. Fourth Edition, revised by a College of Fizz-icians." But, happily for the future propagation of the English-speaking peoples, such meanderings were few and far between.

As the roaring flash fire of erotic literature spread, even reputable biographers, like John Aubrey, the Oxford scholar, indulged themselves in the pastime of writing it. His *Brief Lives,* an uncensored collection of curious items concerning contemporary dignitaries, is like a spy-glass to his time. Look through it and you can see Elizabethan England completely off its guard. The following typical boiled down anecdote comes from his "brief life" of Sir Thomas More:

". . . In his Utopia his law is that the young people are to see each other stark-naked before marriage. Sir William Roper, of Eltham in Kent, came one morning, pretty early, to Sir Thomas, with a proposal to marry one of his daughters. My lord's daughters were then both together abed in a truckle-bed in their father's chamber asleep. He carried Sir William into the chamber and took the sheet by the corner and suddenly whipped it off. They lay on their backs, and their smocks up as high as their armpits. This awakened them, and immediately they turned on their bellies. Quoth Roper, 'I have seen both sides,' and so gave a pat on her buttock he made choice of, saying, 'Thou art mine.'"

Daniel Defoe, the stern 17th century moralist and religious and political pamphleteer, was likewise not without his authorship of the lubric tale. Best known, of course, for his *Robinson Crusoe,* Defoe also wrote *The Fortunate Mistress, Roxana,* and *Moll Flanders.* Indeed, in *Moll Flanders,* Defoe's greatest power as writer is often most clearly seen. Witness his understanding of human frailty in the following passage from *Moll Flanders.* The full title of *Moll Flanders* more or less delineates its plot: *The Fortunes and Misfortunes of the Famous Moll Flanders,* &c., *Who Was Born in Newgate, and During a Life of Continued Variety, For Threescore Years, Besides Her Childhood, Was twelve Years a Whore, Five Times a Wife* (whereof once to her own brother), *Twelve Years a Thief, Eight Years a Transported Felon in Virginia, at Last Grew Rich, lived Honest, and Died a Penitent.*

In the following excerpt, Moll has taken up residence at Bath, where Englishmen often searched for mistresses, rarely for wives. She has just met a man who is separated from his wife and Moll leads him to believe that she herself is a widow. The man is in poor health and has come to the spa to recuperate. Without making any disrespectful overtures, the gentleman asks Moll to serve as his nurse, which she happily assents to do.

"After some time he gathered strength and grew well apace, and I would have removed my pallet-bed, but he would not let me, till he was able to venture himself without anybody to sit up with him, when I removed to my own chamber.

"He took many occasions to express his sense of my tenderness for him; and when he grew well he made me a present of fifty guineas for my care, and, as he called it, hazarding my life to save his.

"And now he made deep protestations of a sincere inviolable affection for me, but with the utmost reserve for my virtue and his own. I told him I was fully satisfied of it. He carried it to that length that he protested to me, that if he was naked in bed with me, he would as sacredly preserve my virtue as he would defend it, if I was assaulted by a ravisher. I believed him, and told him I did so; but this did not satisfy him. He would, he said, wait for some opportunity to give me an undoubted testimony of it.

"It was a great while after this that I had occasion, on my business, to go to Bristol, upon which he hired me a coach, and would go with me; and now indeed our intimacy increased. From Bristol he carried me to Gloucester, which was merely a journey of pleasure, to take the air; and here it was our hap to have no lodgings in the inn, but in one large chamber with two beds in it. The master of the house going with us to show his rooms, and coming into that room, said very frankly to him, 'Sir, it is none of my business to inquire whether the lady be your spouse or no; but if not, you may lie as honestly in these two beds as if you were in two chambers,' and with that he pulls a great curtain which drew quite across the room, and effectually divided the beds. 'Well,' says my friend, very readily, 'these beds will do; and as for the rest, we are too near akin to lie together, though we may lodge near one another,' and this put an honest face on the things too. When we came to go to bed, he decently went out of the room till I was in bed, and then went to bed in the other bed, but lay there talking to me a great while.

"At last, repeating his usual saying, that he could lie naked in the bed with me and not offer me the least injury, he starts out of his bed. 'And now, my dear,' says he, 'you shall see how just I will be to you, and that I can keep my word,' and away he comes to my bed.

"I resisted a little, but I must confess I should not have resisted him much, if he had not made those promises at all. So, after a little struggle, I lay still and let him come to bed. When he was there he took me in his arms, and so I lay all night with him, but he had no more to do with me, or offered anything to me, other than embracing me, as I say, in his arms, no, not the whole night, but rose up and dressed him in the morning, and left me as innocent for him as I was the day I was born.

"This was a surprising thing to me, and perhaps may be so to others, who know how the laws of nature work; for he was a vigorous, brisk person. Nor did he act thus on a principle of religion at all, but of mere affection; insisting on it, that, though I was to him the most agreeable woman in the world, yet, because he loved me, he could not injure me.

"I own it was a noble principle, but as it was what I never saw before, so it was perfectly amazing. We travelled the rest of the journey as we did before, and came back to Bath, where, as he had opportunity to come to me when he would, he often repeated the same moderation, and I frequently lay with him, and although all the familiarities of man and wife were common to us, yet he never once offered to go any farther, and he valued himself much upon it. I do not say that I was so wholly pleased with it as he thought I was, for I own I was much wickeder than he.

"We lived thus near two years, only with this exception, that he went three times to London in that time, and once he continued there four months; but, to do him justice, he always supplied me with money to subsist on very handsomely.

"Had we continued thus, I confess we had had much to boast of; but, as wise men say, it is ill venturing too near the brink of a command. So we found it; and here again I must do him the justice to own that the first breach was not on his part. It was one night that we were in bed together warm and merry, and having drunk, I think, a little more both of us than usual, though not in the least to disorder us, when, after some other follies which I cannot name, and being clasped close in his arms, I told him (I repeat it with shame and horror of soul) that I could find in my heart to discharge him of his engagement for one night and no more.

"He took me at my word immediately, and after that there was no resisting him; neither indeed had I any mind to resist him any more.

"Thus the government of our virtue was broken, and I exchanged the place of friend for that unmusical, harsh-sounding title of whore. In the morning we were both at our penitentials. I cried very heartily, he expressed himself very sorry."

PART III *The Two Manias*

WITH THE ADVENT of the 18th and 19th centuries, English erotica became more and more specialized in its subject matter. Two subjects in particular seemed to dominate: Flagellation and the Defloration of Virgins. Indeed, the emphasis placed on these two themes is what distinguishes English erotica from that of all other languages. It is often said in seriousness that if a scholar were weaned on nothing but erotic reading matter, he would soon come to believe that flagellomania was England's chief cultural pursuit for two hundred years and that the simulation of virginity was the sole object of England's greatest surgical skill.

Of course erotic literature then, as now, was highly topical in nature and the prevalence of these themes in reading matter only reflected the ubiquity of these perversions in real life. For flagellomania in 18th and 19th century England had been cultivated to a degree never before or since equalled by humankind. Pornologic clubs throughout London were fiendishly dedicated to the perpetuation of every conceivable variation of "le vice Anglais," as this pastime was known on the Continent where Frenchmen only half-jokingly referred to the rod as the national symbol of England. Special wooden racks to intensify the so-called ecstacies of the vice were devised, with the most efficient of them named "The Berkeley Horse" in honor of a matron whose finesse with the birch rod was intimately known even in the household of the Crown itself.

Sub rosa magazines like *The Annals of Gallantry, Glee and Pleasure; The Bon Ton Magazine; The Pearl* and the deceptively titled *Englishwoman's Domestic Magazine* gave serious reports of the more spectacular orgies of the day, together with lists of addresses and anatomical specifications of female flagellants available for hire.

Literally thousands of books, brochures and pamphlets were printed on the subject, with *The Whippingham Papers,* to which Swinburne contributed, as probablv the most encyclopedic work on the subject.

"Major Edward Markham," whose real name was Lieutenant St. George H. Stock of the Queen's Royal Regiment, was a prolific writer on the subject, his works including *The Night School, A Dialogue on Stays, The Way To Peel,* and *The Romance of Chastisement.* In 1872 a fictional series on the subject was brought out under title of *The Library Illustrative Of Social Progress,* its separate volumes including *Lady Bumtickler's Revels, A Treatise On the Use Of Flogging In Venereal Affairs,* and *Madam Birchini's Dance.*

Other important works dealing with flagellation were the Howard series (one of the titles in this was *Maud Cameron*), *The Experimental Lecture* and two importations from France, *The Yellow Room* and *Lord Kidrodstick.*

The following passage is a somewhat typical example of erotic writing of this class. It comes from the autobiography of a female flagellant named Margaret Anson titled *The Merry Order Of St. Bridget: Personal Recollections Of The Use Of The Rod.* The extract describes Margaret's initiation into a pornologic club in 1857:

"'Are you, Margaret Anson, prepared to serve the Merry Order to the best of your power, and to assist, as bidden by your mistress, in the ceremonies thereof?'

"'I am.'

"'And do you bind yourself never to reveal aught that you see, hear or do in this room, on peril of losing your place without character?'

"'I do.'

"'Do you know the object of the Merry Order?'

"'I do.'

"'Detail it.'

"Again prompted, I replied, 'The wholesome and pleasant discipline of the rod, to be enforced by its members one upon another during their social meetings in this room.'

"'Have you ever been whipped?'

"'I have.'

"'Do you promise to submit to such flagellation as the Merry Order shall ordain for you without rebellion or murmuring thereat?'

"'I do.'

"'Prepare her.'

"I heard more tittering when this order was given, and I could feel that Mrs. D. . . was shaking with suppressed laughter as she obeyed the command, and took off my peignoir. She pinned up the petticoats and chemise to my shoulders, and then my dear, I knew what was coming. Then some one else took hold of one of my hands, and Mrs. D. . . the other, and waited the word of command.

"'Advance.'

"They led me forward, and at the first step a stinging blow from a birch fell on my hips from one side, then from the other, till I had gone the length of the room. I screamed and struggled, but it was all in vain; my guides held me tight, and by the time they stopped I could only sob and writhe.

"Then came the command, 'Kneel down,' and I knelt in front of the square ottoman; the ladies held my hands across it, and Lady C. . . came down from her dais and whipped me till I hardly knew where I was. Then they made me stand up, and her ladyship said,

"'Ladies of the Order of St. Bridget, do you receive Margaret Anson as a member and servitor sworn to do your bidding?'

"'We do,' said those who were not laughing.

"'Let me see,' was the next order, and at the word one lady let my clothes drop, and the other took the bandage from my eyes. I was so smarting from the whipping I had received, that I could see nothing for a while, and Mrs. D. . . took me by the arm and led me to the bottom of the room again.

"Every lady held a rod in her hand, made of lithe and strong twigs, tied up with ribbons that corresponded with the colours of her dress. On the ottoman over which I had knelt to receive my final castigation lay two more rods.

"'Margaret Anson, approach,' said Lady C. . . once more, and I went timidly forward, wondering whether any more whipping was in store for me.

"'Kneel down.'

"I knelt and she presented me with a rod, and informed me that I was now a servitor of the Merry Order of St. Bridget—allowed to join their ceremonies, and bound to do their bidding; and then I was made to go and stand at the bottom of the room ready to do to the next comer as the ladies had done to me."

As we have observed, flagellation was only one of two grotesqueries that characterized English erotica. The other was the mania for defloration of virgins. This second theme is found running through dozens of books. The authoritative work on the subject is *The Battles of Venus, A Descriptive Dissertation of the Various Modes of Enjoyment of the Female Sex, With Some Curious Information on the Resources of Lust, Lechery and Licentiousness, to Revive the Drooping Faculties and Strengthen the Voluptuous and Exhausted.* Brought out in 1760, it quotes the market price of a "virgo intacto" at fifty pounds and gives the factual account of a lustful old roue who debauched an average of seventy virgins a year over a six year period in a vain attempt to set a world's mark for ravishing one hundred virgins in a single year.

The natural result of this English madness for untouched women was that English bordels were stocked almost exclusively by children, a situation which was not corrected until 1869 when Parliament finally outlawed prostitution as a career for all women under the age of thirteen.

As a literary by-product of all this feverish sensuality, sex manuals made their first appearance in the English language. In marked contrast to our chilly and clinical primers of today, these sex texts taught not so much the biological proficiency of fornication as the variety and gaiety of the act. Their titles reflected this spirit:

How to Raise Love, or the Art of Making Love in More Ways than One.

The Old Man Young Again, or Age Rejuvenescence in the Power of Concupiscence, Being an Excursus on the Uses of Aphrodisiacs and of the Means of Augmenting Carnal Intercourse between the Two Sexes and of Preserving and Giving Greater Force to the Same.

Translations of many foreign sex manuals were also brought into English, enriching even further the fund of sexual know-how of early 19th century England. They included Persia's *The Perfumed Garden* by Sheikh Nefzaui, France's *120 Journees de Sodome* by the Marquis de Sade, which catalogues 600 different perversions, and India's *Kama Sutra* by Vatsya Yana, generally considered the most beautifully and sensually written sex instructor in the world. A glance at *Kama Sutra's* chapter headings gives a clue as to the finesse which it attempts to impart: "Kinds of Sexual Union According to Physical Dimension," "On Biting, Embracing, Kissing, Pressing or Marking with the Nails," "Ways of Love to Be Employed with Women of Different Countries," "Of the Sounds Appropriate to Various Kinds of Congress," "Of Ameliorating Love Quarrels," "Of the Means of Getting Money," and lastly, "Of Signs of Change in a Lover's Feelings and of the Way to Get Rid of Him."

PART IV *London Becomes World Capital*

BY THE 19TH CENTURY, as types of erotica became varied and hundreds of pornographic works had been issued, it was only natural that a central market place for English erotica should be established. And it made its location in Holywell Street in London, named for the "sweete, wholesome and cleere" water of its holy springs. Dozens of the secret presses of England were located in its vicinity and to it came the heirs of England's greatest patrimonies to convert their funds into pornographic libraries. A correspondent to the London *Times* in 1857 described Holywell as "without exception the most vile street in the civilized world, every shop teeming with the most indecent publications and prints."

Along with the establishment of a market place came the first erotic best-sellers, as repeated calls were received for certain books either because of their literary merit or artful salaciousness. Such early standards included:

> The uncensored version of *The Merry Muses of Caledonia: A Collection of Favourite Scot Songs* compiled by Robert Burns, the illustrious Scotch poet.
>
> *Sodom*, by John Wilmot, the Earl of Rochester, who wrote the book as a cynical exposé of debauchery in the Court of Charles II. This book, incidentally, is often thought to have inspired the Marquis de Sade to his literary labors.
>
> *The Toast*, an epic poem in four parts intended to make a whore of a woman who had rejected the love of the author, Dr. William King, a noted theologian and headmaster of Oxford. (It was at Oxford, incidentally, that the inevitable first pornography scandal broke. In 1674 a dozen divinity scholars were caught running off an edition of Aretino's *Figurae Veneris* on the University press.)

The Festival of Love, a collection of 150 ribald and titillating poems comprising over 400 pages.

Finally, a work of classical erotica which is still often reprinted today, *The Lustful Turk. A History Founded on Facts, Containing an Interesting Narrative of the Cruel Fate of the Two Young English Ladies, Named Silvia Carey, and Emily Barlow, Fully Explaining How Emily Barlow, and Her Servant, Eliza Gibbs, on Their Passage to India, Were Taken Prisoners by an Algerine Pirate, and Made a Present Of to the Dey of Algiers; Who, on the Very Night of Their Arrival Debauched Emily.—Containing also, Every Particular of the Artful Plans Laid by the Dey, to Get Possession of the Person of Silvia Carey, Etc., with the Particulars of Her Becoming a Victim to His Libidinous Desires. Which Recital Is also Interspersed with the Histories of Several Other Ladies Confined in the Dey's Harem. One of Which Gives an Account of the Horrid Practises Then Carrying On in Several French and Italian Convents by a Society of Monks, Established at Algiers, under Pretence of Redeeming Christian Slaves; But Who, in Reality, Carried On an Infamous Traffic in Young Girls.—Also an Account of the Sufferings of Eliza Gibbs, from the Flogging Propensities of the Bey of Tunis. With Many Other Curious Circumstances, until the Reduction of Algiers by Lord Exmouth; by Which Means These Particulars Became Known.—The*

Whole Compiled From the Original Letters, By Permission of One of the Sufferers.

But of all standards that have been printed and reprinted again and again, none stands more pre-eminently as the perpetual favorite of English erotica than *Memoirs of the Life of Fanny Hill, or the Memoirs of a Woman of Pleasure*, better known by the name of its heroine, Fanny Hill. The work of a highly educated ex-British Consular official named John Cleland, *Fanny Hill* was written in 1749. Cleland was moved to the effort upon his release from debtor's prison in London when a publisher of smut, using a technique that has since given birth to many of America's best-sellers, offered to rescue him from his penury if only he would write him "a novel of sex, just any kind of novel of sex."

Cleland obliged superbly and *Fanny Hill*, not surprisingly, was an immediate success. Beginning with 1750, edition after edition of it poured forth, not only in the English language, but in almost every other language of the world as well. The French alone gave it a dozen known translations, and the Germans ten. It brought prosperity to scores of publishers, many of whom freely usurped both *Fanny Hill's* title and Cleland's by-line, appending it to works that had nothing at all to do with either. The inevitable bowdlerized version of *Fanny Hill* was brought out within the first year of the book's appearance and it, too, sold well. (Numerous modern reprints of this bowdlerized version, incidentally, continue even now to delude 20th century purchasers into believing they have read the real *Fanny Hill,* when, of course, they have not.) A companion volume to *Fanny Hill,* purporting to be the "male Fanny Hill" was brought out under the title of *Memoirs of a Man of Pleasure,* and it, too, helped along the prosperity of the publishing industry. A bookseller named Griffiths claimed to have made over 10,000 pounds sterling in profits on *Fanny Hill* in its first two years of sale, while Franz von Bayros, the artist, was given a huge emolument to illustrate an edition of it.

In fact, just about everyone connected with the book came off handsomely financially except for John Cleland. All he got was a twenty guinea royalty and boundless heaps of ignominy and scorn for having authored the work. The Privy Council summoned him to answer charges for having written this "excessively sexual" book. Cleland's reply was that he had written it as a work of crusading journalism to expose the degradation of the underworld of sexual vice in his day. If the brothels, bagnios and procuresses in *Fanny Hill* seemed unbelievably crude, argued Cleland, it was only because that's the way they were in real life. Fortunately for Cleland, the President of the Council, the Earl of Granville, was a man of some literary discernment and Cleland was let off with a mere warning to refrain from any such future erotic productions. In fact, to insure Cleland against falling into such financial straights as might tempt him to a repetition of his transgression, the good Earl of Granville awarded Cleland a 100 pound sterling annual pension to cover his cost of living for life!

Cleland was true to the conditions of this government-subsidy-of-the-arts-in-reverse and never again produced anything of the erotic proportions of *Fanny Hill.*

Literati who've read *Fanny Hill* agree that the secret of its popularity lies in the simplicity of its story line and the naturalness with which the debauchery flows from scene to scene. This is in marked contrast to most other erotic fiction where the plots seem almost always to be forced and the heroics somewhat unbelievable.

Specifically, *Fanny Hill* is the familiar story of a young country girl who has come to the big city and it is told in a series of autobiographical letters. Fanny is the daughter of extremely poor parents in a small village near Liverpool. The parents die of smallpox when Fanny is only fifteen and she is beguiled into moving to London by a scheming friend whose real aim is to have her expenses to the big city paid by naive little Fanny. On their arrival in London, the friend vanishes and Fanny is left alone and destitute.

She applies to an employment office and is offered a position in the home of a "Mrs. Brown." Unknown to Fanny, Mrs. Brown is really Madame Brown, the operator of a highly-reputable brothel. The unsuspecting girl is overjoyed at what she considers her good fortune and she accompanies her new mistress to her luxuriously furnished home.

As Mrs. Brown busies herself in finding a purchaser of Fanny's virginity, the girl is entrusted to an affectionate but jaded prostitute named Phoebe Ayres who is supposed to indoctrinate Fanny into the demands of her new calling. But the experienced prostitute is so taken by Fanny's sweet innocence that she takes the country girl for her own pleasure and leads her through a series of lesbian entanglements.

In a few days, Mrs. Brown has found an elderly gentleman who is willing to pay fifty guineas ($250.00) for the privilege of tempting Fanny to sleep with him, with a promise of a one hundred guinea ($500.00) bonus if he succeeds in destroying her virginity. Fanny describes the old cavalier as "a man rather past threescore, short and ill-made, with a yellow cadaverous hue, great goggling eyes, that stared as if he was strangled; an out-mouth for two more properly tusks than teeth, livid lips, and a breath like a jakes'; then he had a peculiar ghastliness in his grin that made him perfectly frightful, if not dangerous to women with child. This then was the monster to which my conscientious benefactress had doomed me.

"She sent for me purposely for his examination. Accordingly she made me stand up before him, turned me around, unpinned my handkerchief, [which appears to have been the extent of Fanny's dishabille], remarked to him the rise and fall, the turn and whiteness of a bosom just beginning to fill; then made me walk, and took even a handle from the rusticity of my charms. In short, she omitted no point of jockeyship, to which he only answered by gracious nods and approbation, whilst he looked goats and monkeys at me."

The elderly gentleman's passion was sufficiently aroused by this exhibition to want to give it a try. But Fanny, still fresh from the country, refuses to submit. After a furious attempt at the seduction, the old rake gives up in disgust.

Soon thereafter, quite by accident, Fanny finds herself witness to an encounter between her procuress, Mrs. Brown, and a young horse grenadier of elephantine venereal proportions who has rented himself to the madame during a portion of his week-end furlough. Fanny is so aroused by the ecstasies she sees that she willingly entrusts herself to the advances of a handsome young man named Charles who is a frequent visitor to Mrs. Brown's seraglio. He helps her escape from the house and brings Fanny to his own lodgings where she willingly yields herself to him in a defloration of prolonged description.

Charles, naturally, is as astonished as he is pleased to discover that Fanny is a true virgin and their mutual regard rapidly develops into ardent love. They set up an elegant apartment and Fanny is insanely happy with Charles:

"Oh, could I paint his figure as I see it now, still present to my transported imagination! a whole length of an all-perfect manly beauty in full view. Think of a face without a fault, glowing with all the opening bloom and verdant freshness of an age, in which beauty is of either sex, and which the first down over his upper lip scarce began to distinguish. The parting of the double ruby pout of his lips seemed to exhale an air sweeter and purer than what it drew in;

ah, what violence did it not cost me to refrain the so tempted kiss! Then a neck exquisitely turned, graced behind and on the sides with his hair, playing freely in natural ringlets, connected his head to a body of the most perfect form, and of the most vigorous context-ure, in which all the strength of manhood was concealed and softened to appearance by the delicacy of his complexion, the smoothness of his skin and the plumpness of his flesh. The platform of his snow white bosom, which was laid out in manly fashion, presented on the vermillion summit of each pap, the idea of a rose about to blow. Nor did his shirt hinder me from observing that symmetry of his limbs, that exactness of shape, in the fall of it towards the loins, where the waist ends and the rounding swell of the hips commences; where the skin, sleek, smooth, and dazzling white, burnishes on the stretchover firm, plump, ripe flesh, that crimped and ran into dimples at the least pressure, or that the touch could not rest upon, but slid over as on the surface of the most polished ivory. . . . His thighs, finely fashioned and with a florid glossy roundness, gradually tapering away to the knees, seemed pillars worthy to support that beauteous frame."

But Fanny's happiness with Charles and his physique is short lived. The affair is discovered by the boy's unreasoning father and Fanny's Apollo is sent away to manage a factory owned by the family in the South Seas.

Fanny, pregnant, is left to her fate. She becomes ill and miscarries. Fanny's landlady, a part-time procuress—as almost everyone who wasn't a full-time lecher seems to have been in those days—puts pressure on the girl to take as a lover a middle-aged man who has coveted her person for some time past, and Fanny acquiesces.

Her sexual life with her new lover is described in great detail. Sensual and passionate, Fanny responds to his love-making physically, but without love. Her satisfaction is nothing compared to the rapture she felt in the arms of Charles. Her new lover installs her in an apartment with a maid and by his repeated kindnesses wins from Fanny a "grateful fondness." She mingles in a circle of wealthy men and their mistresses, and although not happy, is faithful and reasonably content until one day she discovers her man in a tender tete-a-tete with the chambermaid. Fanny resolves to give him tit-for-tat and carries on a liaison with her handsome young livery servant. The lovers are surprised flagrante delicto one day, and Fanny is immediately cast off by her keeper.

With Fanny in this defenseless position, there appears on the scene a brothel-keeper named Mrs. Cole, who is modelled, incidentally, after the notorious real-life Mother Douglas of Covent Garden. She offers Fanny a job in her brothel, and Fanny accepts. Mrs. Cole's place, which is disguised as a milliner's shop, affords a pleasant contrast for Fanny from Mrs. Brown's. "Decency, modesty and order" are the rule, and the girls, only four in number, are pampered and coddled. Under Mrs. Cole's protection and in the company of girls of her own age and inclinations, Fanny passes a pleasant time until her madam, who feels weaknesses coming on with age, decides to retire. Fanny, once more a free-lance, continues her story:

"I had, on my separation from Mrs. Cole, taken a pleasant convenient house at Marlebone, easy to manage for its smallness, which I furnished neatly and modestly. There with a reserve of eight hundred pounds, the fruit of my deference to Mrs. Cole's advice, exclusive of some clothes, jewels, and plate, I saw myself in purse for a long time, to wait without impatience for what the chapter of accidents might produce in my favour. Here under the character of a young gentlewoman whose husband had gone to sea, I had laid out such lines of life and conduct, as leaving me at liberty to pursue my desires, bound me nevertheless strictly within the rules of decency and discretion, a course in which you cannot escape observing as a true pupil of Mrs. Cole's."

Fortune now favors Fanny. She renders first aid to an old gentleman who has been seized by a choking fit, and, in gratitude, he takes her to his home, adopts her, educates her, leaves his fortune to her and then conveniently dies. So our Fanny becomes a great lady and quite her own mistress. She has everything her heart desires, except Charles, whom she has never forgotten.

Taken by a whim to revisit her birthplace, she stops midway at an inn. A sudden storm arises and two horsemen are driven in by the rain. To her infinite joy and delight she recognizes one of the bedraggled figures as none other than her long-lost Charles, who is just returning from his involuntary trip to the South Seas. Financial fortune has not smiled on Charles, but Fanny has enough for the two of them and she places her fortune at his disposal. She also renders him a complete bill of particulars regarding the illicit life she has led in his absence. Charles does not mind. They are legally married and Fanny becomes a good and virtuous housewife.

The story ends with Fanny singing a paean of praise to sexual union *when it is accompanied by love*:

"Thus, at length, I got snug into port, where, in the bosom of virtue, I could not help pitying those who, immersed in gross sensuality, are insensible to the delicate charms of virtue. And if I have painted Vice in all its gayest colours, if I have decked it with flowers, it has been solely in order to make the worthier, the solemner sacrifice of it to Virtue."

In style, *Fanny Hill*, like many another work of classical erotica, is completely devoid of profanity. But it more than makes up for this lack with its recurrent scenes of utmost salaciousness. In addition to scenes already hinted at, there are the voyeuristic activities of Fanny and Mrs. Cole, the young man who has a desire to be flogged, the hair-fetishist, the devices employed for counterfeiting virginity, a transvestite episode, the activities of two homosexuals in a hotel, the vivid narration of their sex histories by the young ladies in Mrs. Cole's brothel and finally the morbid seduction of an idiot boy by one of Fanny's fun-loving girlfriends.

PART V *First American Works*

FANNY HILL is important not only in the history of the erotic literature of England, but of the United States, as well. Copies of *Fanny Hill* were known to exist here even before Freedom of the Press was declared in 1789. In fact, America's first prosecution on obscene literature involved *Fanny Hill*. Two Massachusetts book peddlers were jailed six months apiece in 1821 for tempting rural farmers into purchasing copies of the work.

In 1846 *Fanny Hill* was also responsible for launching the United States on its career as an independent producer of pornography. It was the first work brought out by America's earliest publisher of domestic erotica, William Haynes, a New Yorker and former surgeon from Ireland. Haynes grossed thousands of dollars with *Fanny Hill*, and whereas the United States had always depended upon France and England for its erotic literature—as it had for most of its other tools of scholarship—the profits from *Fanny Hill* now enabled Haynes to bring out 320 other erotic titles.

Fanny Hill's popularity continued right on through the Civil War as it became a barracks favorite and a principal item of stock for sutlers following the troops.

Thanks to Hoe's high-speed press and to the perfection of electrotyped engravings in the post-Civil War period, hundreds of other erotica titles became known to the book-loving public of America. They bore such unmistakably American titles as:

Sodom in Union Square, or Revelations of the Doings in Fourteenth Street. By an ex-Police Captain of New York.

The Lady in Flesh-Coloured Tights.

Amelia Morton: or Life at a Fashionable Watering Place.

Raped on the Elevated Railway. "A true story of a lady who was first ravished, then flagellated on the Uptown Express, illustrating the perils of travel in the new Machine Age."

Flora Montgomerie, the Factory Girl, a Tale of the Lowell Factories, Being a Recital of the Adventures of a Libidinous Millionaire Whose Wealth Was Used as a Means of Triumphing over Virtue.

The Bar Maid of Old Point House, Being the Secret History of the Amours and Intrigues of a Bar Maid Whose Amourous Disposition and Voluptuous Achievements on the Couch of Cupid Made Her the Envy of Her Own Sex and the Admiration of the New World.

The Secret Services and Duties of Major Lovitt, Being a Novel of the Civil War.

John, the Darling of the Philadelphia Ladies.

Compared to the erotic masterpieces of Europe with their morocco bindings, elegant papers and fine illustrations, America's production was, for the most part, a sorry lot. And we were duly taken to task for permitting "only the veriest of grubbians to put their pens at the disposal of Venus and Priapus," as one British bibliographer put it.

What American pornography needed, and needed sorely, was for one of its great authors to put his hand to writing erotica and come up with a work that would save his country's honor in the international race to inflame the non-political passions of mankind.

Mark Twain was the author who arose to the occasion and his masterpiece, which is still little known outside of bibliophilic circles, was *1601 . . . Conversation as It Was by the Social Fireside in the Time of the Tudors.* Twain wrote it in the summer of 1876, as he was about to finish *Tom Sawyer*, a work intended for a younger generation of American males, and as he was about to start *The Adventures of Huckleberry Finn.*

Representing Twain's richest expression of contempt for overstuffed language and the idiocies of convention, *1601* is a suppostitious conversation at the fireside of Queen Elizabeth that takes place in the year 1601. The protagonists are the good Queen, several literary dignitaries, and one or two members of the court. Someone in the room has just given vent to a monstrous flatulance, completely disrupting the social gathering, and the conversation centers around the anonymous manufacturer of the scent. The Queen queries her guests to determine the issuer of this aeolian crepitation. Ben Jonson, Beaumont, the Duchess of Bilgewater and William "Shaxpur" in turn all deny authorship of the scent, with Shaxpur paying it due tribute in a line to the effect that "Heaven's artillery hath shook ye globe in admiration of it."

Finally, in order that the conversation may move on to a discussion of extra-marital fornication within the Queen's court, gallant old Sir Walter Raleigh takes the blame for having broken wind, though, in truth, it was the Queen's cup-bearer who had emitted the stench.

Easily as scatological as it is sexual, *1601* gave Twain, the bad boy of American literature, an opportunity to employ almost every verbal indecency of the English language. And he took full advantage of the opportunity. "If there is a decent word findable in it," he once wrote to a Cleveland librarian, "it is because I overlooked it."

Many years later, Twain revealed that he had written *1601* for the delectation of his closest friend, the Reverend Joseph Twichell of Asylum Hill Congregational Church, Hartford, Conn. Reverend Twichell had known Twain for over forty years and had presided over Twain's wedding and solemnized the births of all his children. The book first came to be printed when another friend of Twain's, John Hay, who later became Secretary of State, saw the work and had four copies of it put in pamphlet form in 1880.

1601's first printing as a hard-cover book took place two years later at—of all places—the United States Military Academy at West Point. There, still another friend of Twain's, Lieutenant C. E. S. Wood, had charge of the Academy's printing press and ran through an elegant edition of fifty copies on handmade linen paper. They were distributed to popes, kings and other such dignitaries as far off as Japan, where *1601* remains today far more popular and better known than it is in its native land. In all, *1601* has gone through some forty-four editions here in the United States, with scores of others in foreign languages overseas.

1601's acclaim among the cognoscenti of the book world, even before it was in book form, paved the way for Twain to visit the secret treasure vaults of the Berlin Royal Library during his celebrated trip abroad. There he was able to peruse the Kaiser's pornographic holdings with the greatest of freedom, as he has recorded in his writings. *1601* also secured for him an invitation to address the Stomach Club in Paris where his topic was "Some Remarks on the Science of Onanism."

And so it was that the United States became a power to be reckoned with in the world of pornographic letters thanks to this curious masterpiece from the pen of America's greatest literary wit.

Scholars of erotic literature know, of course, that Benjamin Franklin had written a scatalogical masterpiece almost a hundred years before Twain wrote 1601. Franklin's effort was in the form of a letter to the Royal Academy of Brussels outlining his plan to convert the offensive odor of flatulence into sweet smelling aromas by the addition of chemical powders to food. But the Franklin letter was not published until one hundred and fifty years after it was written and so the distinction of having published America's first erotic masterpiece belongs to Twain.

The Franklin letter, interesting because it indicates the range of Franklin's interests as an inventor, now reposes among the Franklin papers at the Library of Congress. It is herewith printed in full:

"Gentlemen:

"I have perused your late mathematical prize question, proposed in lieu of one in natural philosophy for the ensuing year. . . . I conclude therefore that you have given this question instead of a philosophical, or, as the learned express it, a *physical* one, because you could not at the time think of a physical one that promised greater *utility*. . . . Permit me then humbly to propose one of that sort for your consideration, and through you, if you approve it, for the serious inquiry of learned physicians, chemists, etc., of this enlightened age.

"It is universally well known that, in digesting our common food, there is created or produced in the bowels of human creatures a great quantity of wind.

"That the permitting this air to escape and mix with the atmosphere is usually offensive to the company, from the fetid smell that accompanies it.

"That all well-bred people, therefore, to avoid giving such offense, forcibly restrain the efforts of nature to discharge that wind.

"That so retained contrary to nature it not only gives frequently great present pain, but occasions future diseases such as habitual cholics, ruptures, tympanies, etc., often destructive of the constitution, and sometimes of life itself.

"Were it not for the odiously offensive smell accompanying such escapes, polite people would probably be under no more restraint in discharging such wind in company than they are in spitting or in blowing their noses.

"My prize question therefore should be: To discover some drug, wholesome and not disagreeable, to be mixed with our common food, or sauces, that shall render the natural discharges of wind from our bodies not only inoffensive, but agreeable as perfumes.

"That this is not a chimerical project and altogether impossible, may appear from these considerations. That we already have some knowledge of means capable of *varying* that smell. He that dines on stale flesh, especially with much addition of onions, shall be able to afford a stink that no company can tolerate; while he that has lived for some time on vegetables only, shall have that breath so pure as to be insensible to the most delicate noses; and if he can manage so as to avoid the report, he may anywhere give vent to his griefs, unnoticed. But as there are many to whom an entire vegetable diet would be inconvenient, and as a little quicklime thrown into a jakes will correct the amazing quantity of fetid air arising from the vast mass of putrid matter contained in such places, and render it rather pleasing to the smell, who knows but that a little powder of lime (or some other thing equivalent), taken in our food, or perhaps a glass of limewater drunk at dinner, may have the same effect on the air produced in and issuing from our bowels? This is worth the experiment. Certain it is also that we have the power of changing by slight means the smell of another discharge, that of our water. A few stems of asparagus eaten shall give our urine a disagreeable odor; and a pill of turpentine no bigger than a pea shall bestow on it the pleasing smell of violets. And why should it be thought more impossible in nature to find means of making perfume of our wind than of our water?

"For the encouragement of this inquiry (from the immortal honor to be reasonably expected by the inventor), let it be considered of how small importance to mankind, or to how small a part of mankind have been useful those discoveries in science that have heretofore made philosophers famous. Are there twenty men in Europe, this day the happier, or even the easier, for any knowledge they have picked out of Aristotle? What comfort can the vortices of Descartes give to a man who has whirlwind in his bowels! The knowledge of Newton's mutual *attraction* of the particles of matter, can it afford ease to him who is racked by their mutual *repulsion,* and the cruel distensions it occasions? The pleasure arising to a few philosophers, from seeing, a few times in their lives, the threads of light untwisted, and separated by a Newtonian prism into seven colors, can it be compared with the ease and comfort every man living might feel seven times a day, by discharging freely the wind from his bowels? Especially if it be converted into a perfume; for the pleasures of one sense being little inferior to those of another, instead of pleasing the *sight,* he might delight the *smell* of those about him, and make numbers happy, which to a benevolent mind must afford infinite satisfaction. The generous soul, who now endeavors to find out whether the friends he entertains like best claret or Burgundy, champagne or Madeira, would then inquire also whether they chose musk or lily, rose or bergamot, and provide accordingly. And surely such a liberty of *ex-pressing one's scentiments,* and pleasing one another, is of infinitely more importance to human happiness than that liberty of the *press,* or of *abusing one another,* which the English are so ready to fight and die for.

"In short, this invention, if completed, would be as Bacon expresses it, *bringing philosophy home to men's business and bosoms.* And I cannot but conclude that in comparison therewith for *universal* and *continual utility,* the science of the philosophers abovementioned, even with the addition, gentlemen, of your '*figure quelconque,*' and the figures inscribed in it, are all together, scarcely worth a

Fart-hing"

Of course the output of American erotica—and, for that matter, that of any of the English-speaking people—has by no means been limited strictly to books and printed material. The leading lights of both painting and lyric music in Britain and America have also lent their talents to creating erotica. In painting, this has included such names as Hogarth, Rowlandson and Aubrey Beardsley, though of course they do not even begin to compare in stature with masters of the continent like Rubens, Rembrandt, Jan Steen, Michelangelo, Raphael, Tintoretto, Titian, Boucher and Rodin whose secret works also depict erotic scenes.

In music, no lesser two personages than Messrs.

Gilbert and Sullivan are found to have created musical erotica. Their magnum opus was an obscene opera called *The Sod's Opera,* which included the characters of Count Tostoff, The Brothers Bollox, a pair of hangers on, and Scrotum, a wrinkled old retainer. Sir Arthur Sullivan, it will be remembered, also composed dozens of Christianity's most passionate hymns, including *Onward Christian Soldiers.*

As may be observed, the type of erotica which is intended as a substitute for sex rather than as a commentary upon it, has always flourished in times when society imposed its harshest restrictions upon sexual expression. It is not surprising, therefore, to find a sharp drop-off in the output of English and American erotica as we round the corner of the 20th century. In fact, since Henry Miller's stature as a literary figure is still a matter of heated debate, only two modern writers remain as authors of importance in erotica. The first is Frank Harris and the second is D. H. Lawrence.

Lawrence's chef d'oeuvre was, of course, the unexpurgated *Lady Chatterley's Lover* brought out in 1928. It is not only the finest erotic novel ever written in the English language, but probably the best ever written in any language. Characteristically insular in its poignancy, it tells the story of a woman whose husband, Sir Clifford Chatterley, is hopelessly paralyzed "from the hips down." To alleviate her sexual frustrations, the woman, Lady Constance Chatterley, takes up with her husband's game-keeper, Oliver Mellors, a robust "rush of a man."

The affair is at first sporadic and clandestine. As Lady Chatterley becomes more and more involved with Mellors, however, she asks her paralyzed husband for a divorce. He refuses. Lady Chatterley takes the only way out: she defies convention and decides to live with Mellors despite her huband's refusal.

Sir Clifford Chatterley is, of course, symbolic of the emotional paralysis of his class and of men like him. Lawrence expands upon the message of his story in the introduction to the privately printed unexpurgated Paris edition of *Lady Chatterley's Lover*:

"The great necessity is that we should act according to our thoughts, and think according to our acts. And this is the real point of this book. I want men and women to be able to *think* sex, fully, completely, honestly and cleanly. Even if we can't *act* sexually to our complete satisfaction, let us at least think sexually, complete and clear."

What Lawrence is striving for ultimately is a reconciliation between man's thoughts about sex, as tempered by society, and his instincts, as provided by nature. Evidences of Lawrence's hopefulness of attaining this goal appear throughout *Lady Chatterley's Lover*. The following excerpt in which Lady Constance Chatterley and Mellors commune with Mother Earth is typical:

"She opened the door and looked at the straight heavy rain, like a steel curtain, and had a sudden desire to rush into it, to rush away. She got up, and began swiftly pulling off her stockings, then her dress and underclothing, and he held his breath. Her pointed keen animal breasts tipped and stirred as she moved. She was ivory-coloured in the greenish light. She slipped on her rubber shoes again and ran out with a wild little laugh, holding up her breasts to the heavy rain and spreading her arms, and running blurred in the rain with the eurythmic dance-movements she had learned so long ago in Dresden. It was a strange pallid figure lifting and falling, bending so the rain beat and glistened on the full haunches swaying up again and coming belly-forward through the rain then stooping again so that only the full loins and buttocks were offered in a kind of homage towards him, repeating a wild obeisance.

"He laughed wryly, and threw off his clothes. It was too much. He jumped out, naked and white, with a little shiver, into the hard slanting rain. Flossie sprang before him with a frantic little bark. Connie, her hair all wet and sticking to her head, turned her hot face and saw him. Her blue eyes blazed with excitement as she turned and ran fast, with a strange charging movement, out of the clearing and down the path, the wet boughs whipping her. She ran, and he saw nothing but the round wet head, the wet back leaning forward in flight, the rounded buttocks twinkling: a wonderful cowering female nakedness in flight."

Lawrence's outcry for freedom of thought and expression of sex extends to free usage of the language of sex, too. This includes use of even the most rigidly tabooed words, two of which he sprinkles liberally throughout his book. Naturally, this shocked a number of people when *Lady Chatterley's Lover* was brought out and raised quite a bit of condemnation for the book, to which Lawrence replied:

"The words that shock so much at first don't shock at all after a while. People without minds may go on being shocked, but they don't matter. People with minds realize that they aren't shocked, and never really were."

As we have noted, the second important erotic writer of the 20th century is Frank Harris. His book is *My Life and Loves,* an autobiography marked by the faithfulness and intimacy with which the author has reported his own sex adventures.

Harris' varied occupations and wide travels during his life gave him plenty of opportunty to meet fascinating women, first as a youth in Ireland, then as a bridge-builder, rancher, hotel clerk, land speculator, and lawyer in the United States, next as a Moscow correspondent in the Russian-Turkish War, then as a professor and newspaperman in England, and finally as a wandering student of life at Heidelberg, Athens, Rome, Constantinople, Vienna, Italy and the French Riviera. And Harris never failed to exploit to the fullest the female contacts he made along the way of this pilgrimage through life.

To date, *My Life and Loves* has been issued in four volumes, with a fifth volume covering the last years of Harris' life as yet unpublished because women involved in it are still alive. Harris died at Nice in 1931 at the age of seventy-five. Typical of his sex adventures is a scene which takes place when he and his gardener contrive to run a beauty contest among girls of the villa in San Remo where Harris is then residing. Rules of the contest require the girls to strip in order to be judged for the five prizes, which range from 100 francs for the first place to twenty-five for third.

Five girls compete in all and each is placed in a separate bedroom. Harris and the Italian gardener go from room to room to appraise the raw features of their contestants. As they enter the room of the third contestant, Harris says:

"There I had one of the surprises of my life: a girl stood on a rug near the bed with the color coming and going in her cheeks; she was in her shirt but with her dress held round her hips. She said she didn't want to strip—she would rather go home.

"'But nothing has happened to you,' said the gardener, 'surely a couple of men to admire you isn't going to make you angry; and that frown doesn't suit your loveliness at all.'

"In two or three minutes the wily Italian gardener had dissipated her anger and she began to smile, and suddenly shrugging her shoulders she put down the dress and then at once stood up at his request, trying to laugh. She had one of the loveliest figures and faces that I ever saw in my life. Her breasts were small, but beautifully rounded and strangely firm; her hips, too, and bottom were as firm as marble, but a little slight. Her face was lit up with a pair of great hazel eyes and her mouth, though a little large, was perfectly formed; her smile won me. I told the gardener that I didn't want to see any more girls, that I was quite content; and he encouraged me to kiss and talk to her while he went into the next room to see the next applicant.

"As soon as the gardener left the room, my beauty, whose name was Flora, began questioning me: 'Why did you choose me? You are the owner, aren't you?' I could only nod. I had sense enough to say, 'partly for your beauty; but also because I like you, your ways, your courage.'

"'But,' she went on, 'real liking does not grow as quickly as that, or just by the view of a body and legs.'

"'Pardon me,' I rejoined, 'but passion, desire in a man comes first: it's for the woman to transform it into enduring affection. You like me a little because I admire and desire you; it's for me by kindness and sympathy to turn that liking into love; so kiss me and don't let us waste time arguing. Can you kiss?'

"'Of course I can,' she said, 'every one can!'

"'That's not true,' I retorted, 'the majority of virgins can't kiss at all, and I believe you're a virgin.'

"'I am,' she replied; 'but you'll not find many in this crowd.'

"'Kiss me,' I went on, taking her in my arms and kissing her till I found response in hot lips. As she used her tongue, she asked roguishly, 'Well, Sir, can I kiss?'

"'Yes,' I replied; 'and now I'll kiss you.'

"Suddenly she started up and danced around me in her fascinating nudity, 'shall I have a prize?'

"'The first,' I cried.

"'Carissimo mio,' and she kissed me a dozen times, 'I'll be whatever you want and cover you with love.'

"Our talk had gone on for perhaps half an hour when a knock came at the door, and the gardener came in to find us both quite happy and, I think, intimately pleased with each other."

In addition to supplying commentary and insight into his own sex life, Harris has included in *My Life and Loves* numberless mordant observations on the private affairs of Shakespeare, Queen Victoria, Prince Edward, and Lord Randolph Churchill. Many of these were celebrities with whom he came in contact as editor of the *London Evening News*. Shaw and Mencken were wild for *My Lives and Loves* and praised it lavishly. A New York judge named Levy, on the other hand, thought it was "not only obviously and unquestionably obscene, lewd, lascivious and indecent, but also filthy disgusting and utterly revolting."

Harris himself, in sitting down to write *My Life and Loves,* stated that he wanted the book to tell "the truth and nothing but the truth" about himself and others and that he would be "at least as kindly to others as to myself." Accordingly, Harris never permitted a volume of his autobiography to be issued while any of the women involved in it were still alive.

Unfortunately, the world in general and the book trade in particular were not nearly as charitable to

Harris. He had to put up his own money to see an edition of his book committed to print, and even so the job had to be done in France because no English or American printer would touch the work. Two expurgated editions of Harris' work appeared later, however, both printed in the United States following Harris' death. One rigorously deletes any reference whatever to sex. The other expunges everything *but* Harris' sex escapades.

PART VI *Reference Works*

LITERARY SHENANIGANS of the sort suffered by *My Life and Loves* have not made the bibliography of erotic works an easy task. On the contrary, erotic bibliography is generally considered the most heavily obstructed pursuit in the field of library science. This is due mainly to the fact that erotic books are generally published in private editions, in limited numbers, and for such obscure circles of fanciers as the Society of Private Bibliophiles of Philadelphia,

The Erotica Bibliomaniac Society and the Society of Vice of London, and the Esoterika Biblion Society of New York. By-lines are contrived, titles are deliberately cast into foreign languages, misleading imprimatures are affixed, and cities and dates of publication are falsified.

And yet despite these enormous difficulties, about a dozen of the most beautiful and tenderly-compiled bibliographies in the English language concern the field of erotic literature. They represent literally hundreds of years of research. The most recent is *Registrum Librorum Eroticorum,* issued in 1936 and compiled by "Rolf S. Reade," the pseudonym of an English booklorist named Alfred Rose. It lists over 5,000 English, French, German and Italian titles.

Older such tomes are the *Index Librorum Prohibitorum,* whose title is stolen from the list of reading matter proscribed to Catholics, the *Centuria Librorum Absconditorum,* and *Catena Librorum Tacendorum,* all by Henry Spencer Ashbee. Ashbee, who used the nom de plume "Pisanus Fraxi," is unquestionably the foremost English erotic bibliographer of all time. His private erotic library, which is now owned by the British Museum, was appraised at over one million dollars at the time of his death in 1900.

Apart from bibliographies, other works of reference include thesauruses like Pierre Pierrugues' *Glossarium Eroticum,* and dictionaries that define words which would otherwise be meaningless to the uninitiated.

Delveau's *Dictionnaire erotique, The Whore's*

Rhetorick, and John Bee's *Sportman's Slang* are typical of such dictionaries, with Captain Grose's *A Classical Dictionary of the Vulgar Tongue* as the heavy on the subject. Definitions from them are not only edifying, but amusing:

ANKLE—a pregnant girl is said to have "sprained her ankle."

ARMOUR—to fight in—to use a condom.

BROTHER STARLING—One who sleeps with the same girl.

COFFEEHOUSE—Prolonged or interrupted coitus.

FACEMAKING—Coitus.

GAP-STOPPER—Bordel madam.

INDORSER—Pederast.

RIDING ST. GEORGE—Coitus inversus.

As has been pointed out, the ballads of the English language with their libidinous scorn and Rabelaisianism are rich in eroticism. Researchers in this particular field have found the following five source books especially handy:

The Roxburghe Ballads, reprinted by The Ballad Society (London), in eight volumes, 1869-80, edited by William Chappell and J. W. Ebsworth

Choyce Drollery: Songs & Sonnets, edited by J. W. Ebsworth, Boston, 1886

Merry Songs and Ballads, edited by J. S. Farmer, 1897, in five volumes, privately printed

A Second Collection of the Newest and Most Ingenious Poems, Satyrs, Songs &c against Popery, London, 1689

The Common Muse, Edited by Vivian de Sola Pinto and Allan Edwin Rodway, The Philosophical Library, New York, 1957, in Limited Edition, with special Appendices

The following two ballads are characteristic of those found in these collections. The first is from volume two of *The Roxburghe Ballads,* the original broadside of which is in the British Museum. The ballad tells the classic tale of the maiden reclining in the hay who suddenly finds herself spied upon by a young shepherd. The ballad also ends in the traditional way:

THE COY SHEPHERDESS

Fair Phillis in a wanton posture lyes,
Not thinking to be seen by mortall eyes
Till accidentally Amintas came,
And see her lye, which made her blush for shame;
He cast himself down by her on the hay,
And won her love before he went away.

Phillis on the new made hay
On a pleasant Summers day
She in wanton posture lay
  thinking no Shephard nigh her
Till Amintas came that way
  and threw himself down by her.

At first she was amaz'd
And with blushes on him gaz'd
Her beauty bright did him invite
  her shape he did admire,
Her wanton dress could do no less,
  then set his heart on fire

Then Amintas mildly said,
Phillis be not now afraid
But entertain thy shepherd swain,
  now we are met together,
Then I shall prize thy sparkling eyes
  that did invite me hither.

I have rang'd the plains about
For to find my Phillis out
My flocks I left, of joys bereft,
  whilst I for thee did languish;
Tis in thy will my heart to fill
  with joy or else with anguish.

Then fair Phillis frowning said,
My privacy thou hast betraid;
Therefore be gone, let me alone,
  do not disturb my pleasure,
Nor do not move thy sute of love,
  but leave me to my leasure.

Never yet did Shepheards Swain
On this smooth Sicilian plain
Once dare to move my deep disdain
  by such like bold intrusion,
Then cease thy suit, 'tis but in vain
  I scorn such fond delusion.

When Amintas see her frown
Hoping still his joys to crown
Quoth he my dear, as I am here
  I like not this behaviour;
Tis lovers bliss, to toy and kiss
  it wins a maidens favor.

Let us like the Ivy twine
And our lives in one combine
Grim Pluto loved Proserpine
  her beauty did him fetter;
When thou art mine and I am thine,
  I'le please thee ten times better.

Fye for shame fond boy, she said,
I'm resolv'd to live a Maid,
Thou art too young, to do me wrong
  be not so bold to venture,
Whilst he poor youth, to speak the truth,
  still aimed at the center.

Phillis blusht as red as blood
When his mind she understood
His bold intent for to prevent,
  she us'd her best endeavor,
His resolution it was bent
  for he was loath to leave her.

Hotly he persued the Game,
Whilst his heart was on a flame
She cry'd Pish nay fye for shame
  in faith you shall not do it
But the youth her overcame
  and eagerly fell to it.

Thus she strived all in vain
Whilst she felt a pleasing pain,
Yet he by no means would refrain
  but kindly did imbrace her,
He kist his love and told her plain
  he never would disgrace her.

In great rage she flung away
Tumbling ore the new-made hay
Whilst he ashamed and breathless lay;
  although he then displeased her,
He rally'd and renewd the fray,
  and manfully appeas'd her.

Thus they spent this christal day
In such wanton sports and play,
Amintas there, imbrac'd his Dear,
  and bid her be lighthearted;
But night being come they hasted home,
  and kindly kist and parted.

The intent, rough and tumble sensuality of ballads like the foregoing *The Coy Shepherdess* leave little room for wit and humor. But that is not to say that all erotic ballads are lacking in drollery. On the contrary. The humor and levity of ballads like *The Unfortunate Miller* are so marked as to relegate the sensuality of the ballad itself to almost laughable importance. *The Unfortunate Miller,* like *The Coy Shepherdess,* appears also in its original broadside in the British Museum. Here it is:

THE UNFORTUNATE MILLER

All of you that desire to hear a jest,
Come listen a while and it shall be exprest;
It is of a Miller that lived very near,
The like of this ditty you never did hear,
A handsome young Damsel she came to his Mill,
To have her Corn Ground with Ready good Will,
As soon as he saw her beauty so bright,
He caused this young Damosel to tarry all night.

Said he, my dear Jewel, it will be ne'r Morn,
Before my Man Lawrence can grind my Dears Corn,
And therefore if thou wilt be ruled by me,
At home in my Parlour thy Lodging shall be,
For I am inflam'd with thy Amorous Charms,
And therefore this Night thou shalt sleep in my arms,
I swear it, and therefore it needs must be so,
It is but in vain for to answer me no.

At this the young Damsel she blushing did stand,
But strait ways the Master took her by the hand,
And leading her home to young Gillian his wife,
Said he, my sweet honey, the joy of my Life,
Be kind to this Maid, for her Father I know,
And let her lye here in the Parlour below,
Stout Lawrence my servant, and I, we shall stay
All night in the Mill till the dawning of Day.

To what he desired she straitways agreed,
And then to the Mill did he hasten with speed,
He ready was then to leap out of his skin,
To think of the Bed which he meant to Lye in;
Now when he was gone, the Maid told his intent,
To Gillian, and they a new Project invent,

By which they well fitted his Crafty young blade;
The Miller by Lawrence a Cuckold was made.

The Maid and his Wife they changed Bed for that night,
So that when the Miller came for his delight,
Strait way to the Parlour Bed he did Repair,
Instead of the Damsel wife Gillian was there,
Which he did Imagine had been the young Lass,
When after some hours in pleasure they past,
He ris, and return'd to the Mill, like one wild,
For fear he had Got the young Damsel with child.

Then to his man Lawrence the miller did say,
I have a young damsel both bonny and Gay,
Her Eyes are like diamonds, her cheeks sweet and fair,
They may with the Rose and the Lilly Compare,
Her lips they are like the rich coral for Red,
This Lass is at home in my Parlour a Bed,
And if you go home you may freely enjoy,
With her the sweet pleasure, for she is not Coy.

His masters kind Proffer he did not refuse,
But was brisk and Airy, and pleased with the News,
But said, to your self much beholding I am,
And for a Requital i'le give you my Ram;
This done lusty Lawrence away home he goes,
And stript off his Coat, Breeches, likewise shooes and hose,
And went into Bed to Gillian his dame,
Yet Lawrence for this was not worthy of blame.

He little Imagen'd his Dame was in bed,
And therefore his heart was the freeer from dread,
The minutes in Pastime and pleasure they spent,
Unknown to them both she injoy'd true content,
Now after a while he his dame had imbrac'd,

He Rose and Returned to the mill in all hast,
Telling his master of all the delight,
Which he had enjoyed with the damsel this Night.

Next morning the maid to the mill did Repair,
The miller and Lawrence his servant was there,
His master then whisper'd this word in her Ear,
How like you to lye with a miller, my dear?
At this the young damsel then laughing out Right;
And said I chang'd Beds with young Gillian last Night;
If you enjoyed any it was your sweet wife,
For my part I ne'r lay with man in my Life.

At this he began for to Rave, stamp and stare,
Both scratching his Elbows and Hauling his hair,
And like one distracted about he did Run,
And oftentimes Crying, ha! what have I done,
Was ever poor miller so finely betrayed,
By Lawrence my man, I am Cuckold made,
The damsel she laught, and was pleased in her mind,
And said he was very well served in his kind.

Apart from the field of balladry, other erotic reference works include, *Scatologic Rites of All Nations,* by Captain John G. Bourke of the 3rd Cavalry, and two important collections of erotic limericks. The first, *Some Limericks,* is ascribed to Norman Douglas, the modern British author, and was privately printed in Florence in 1928. The second book, *The Limerick,* believed to have been edited by Gershon Legman, an American living in France, was brought out there in 1953. It contains the impressive total of 1,700 erotic rhymes. Only two copies of it are known to have been smuggled into the United States thus far.

Typical of the limericks to be found in these collections are the following five:

A niece of the late Queen of Sheba
Was promiscuous with an amoeba.
  This queer blob of jelly
  Would lie in her belly
And, quivering, murmur: "Ich Liebe!"

There was a pert lass from Madras
Who had a remarkable ass—
  Not rounded and pink,
  As you probably think.
It was gray, had long ears and ate grass.

There was a young actress named Ransom
Who was raped seven times in a hansom.
  When she clamored for more
  Came a voice from the floor,
"The name, ma'am, is Simpson—not Samson."

Have you heard about Madam Lupescu,
Who came to Rumania's rescue?
  It's a wonderful thing
  To be under a king.
Is democracy better? I eskyou?

There was a young lady named Banker,
Who slept while her ship lay at anchor.
  She awoke in dismay
  When she heard the mate say:
"Hi! Hoist up the top-sheet and spanker!"

Scarcer in the United States even than Legman's limerick book, however, is another work of reference, an eleven volume encyclopedia of sexual knowledge of which only one copy is known to exist in the United States. It is titled *My Secret Life* and runs to 4,000 pages. Compiled by an anonymous but exceedingly wealthy Englishman, and printed in 1888 in an edition of just six copies, it describes every known form of sexual perversion, from lesbianism, pederasty and flagellomania to sodomy, incest and bestiality. The extensiveness of the work is indicated by the 223 subheadings under "Copulation" to be found in its index.

When the one known American copy of this work changed hands some twenty-six years ago, the price was said to have been $7,000.00 The compiler of the encyclopedia claimed to have personally tested all sexual aberrations described therein, which may help to explain why the work reads much more like a series of hastily jotted notations than does, for example, the *Encyclopaedia Britannica.*

The reference works on erotic art are, in their own way, even more fascinating than those of literature. Essentially they are collections of voluptuous illustrations by Europe's great masters of painting. The little text that accompanies them is almost always in German, a tongue noted for its scientific precision and lack of erotic colloquiality.

Two German sexologists, Eduard Fuchs and Dr. Iwan Bloch, are mainly responsible for the works in this field. Fuchs' *Titanen Erotik,* which measures two feet by four feet and reproduces the secret works of the great masters in color, is certainly the most magnificent work from point of production. The most complete, however, is the *Bilderlexicon,* a four volume work illustrating the dynamics of sexual performance arranged from A to Z. Source material for it came from over 100,000 illustrations, many from the great library of the Institut für Sexualwissenschaft of Berlin. The disappearance of this library under Hitler remains one of the great mysteries of the erotic book world and a loss often compared to the burning of the Alexandrian Library.

The whereabouts of the world's remaining great collections of erotica, though unknown to the public at large, is of course no great secret to bibliographers and librarians.

The world's foremost collection reposes in the Library of the Vatican, in Rome. It includes 25,000 volumes and some 100,000 prints, collected over the centuries from all parts of the world as specimen outcroppings of the creative urge that are to be shunned by good Catholics.

The world's second largest erotic collection is held by the British Museum in London. As noted, Henry Spencer Ashbee's private library forms its nucleus, and its total holdings come to 20,000 volumes. In addition, the British Museum collection embraces a number of curious erotic objets d'art, including a photograph of Algernon Swinburne, the poet, intimately engaged with a buxom young American actress who posed for the shot while on a good-will tour of the British Isles.

The world's third ranking collection of erotica

was started by the late Dr. Alfred C. Kinsey at Indiana University's Institute for Sex Research. The size of Dr. Kinsey's collection—some 15,000 volumes—represents a remarkable feat of American ingenuity in view of the fact that it was started only some fifteen years ago. In fact, so rapidly has the Kinsey collection been assembled that much of its material is as yet uncatalogued, a task for which the Institute is not lacking in learned volunteers.

The Kinsey collection also includes a great deal of artwork, ranging in media of expression from latrine wall scrawlings to several great masterpieces on canvas which New York's Metropolitan Museum of Art has been longing to acquire. Also in the Sex Institute's possession is an array of Japanese "pillow books" —illustrated sex manuals that are kept close at hand by Japanese newlyweds—and a lovely collection of Peruvian sex pottery.

Fixing the relative importance of world collections of erotica beyond Dr. Kinsey's becomes largely a matter of conjecture. Each collection has its characteristics that make comparisons difficult. The Bibliotheque Nationale in Paris, for example, is noted not so much for its size—a mere 2,500 volumes—as for the excellence of its editions. The same is true for the personal collection of the late J. P. Morgan, who spent over a million dollars for his bejewelled, illuminated manuscripts. The Library of Congress in Washington, which owns some 5,000 erotic works, includes many editions taken as Post Office and Customs seizures which are unique in this country. Medical school and psychiatric libraries are also repositories of erotica, though they tend more to collect works of manifest aberration than of literary merit. Among such leading medical libraries are those of the New York Academy of Medicine and the New York State Psychiatric Institute, the latter which snatched the personal library of Sigmund Freud from under the Nazis' nose in 1939 when Freud fled to England.

As for private collections, most of those in America today were started by the financial barons of the 19th century. They remain, for the most part, in the hands of heirs, as divorce testimony periodically bears up, though some of the finest have been turned over to colleges. The Ivy League schools, which have always stressed the value of a liberal education, seem to have been especially well-favored with such benefaction. In the West, the pre-eminent collection of erotica was owned by Henry E. Huntington, California's great railroad and real estate promoter, and is now housed in the library and museum named for him at San Marino, California.

King Farouk was thought for many years to possess an important private collection of erotica, but when he fled to Capri in abdication and his palace was opened to the press, the collection was found to be nothing but a monumental heap of cheap pin-up slides, novelty drinking glasses, and crude home movies.

It is interesting to note here that no woman has ever been known to own an important collection of erotica, despite Dr. Kinsey's statistics which indicate that women are just as easily titillated by erotica's charms as men.

Lest the reader of this essay be misled into believing that mere possession of erotic collections by public or quasi-public libraries guarantees their access to the average reader, it must be pointed out here that such is not the case, even when such libraries are supported by public funds.

On the contrary, most of the libraries mentioned here will open their erotic books only to the most highly-qualified scholars, bearing unimpeachable credentials as to the nature of their projects. The layman requesting a casual look-see at the sex works in any of these libraries would most likely end up with one of several standard library pretexts designed to throw him off the scent.

A blushing, stuttering, almost hysterical librarian will tell him, for example, that "no such collection exists here," or that "we gave those books away years ago." Or, the librarian may confess that the library does own "half a dozen or so obscene works" and then bring forth such racy specimens as the Studs Lonigan trilogy, an expurgated *Decameron,* and a World War I manual on social disease designed to keep the American Expeditionary Forces out of trouble in France.

Nor need the casual reader try finding erotic works listed in the libraries' catalogues. In almost all cases, their cards are kept in special under-the-counter trays with no references to them whatever in the main catalogue, a procedure which has materially hurt many a serious scholarly project. The New York Public Library even has erotic works which it does not list in its restricted catalogue!

The names which libraries give to their erotica collections are an index of the discomfort and terror with which they handle such materials. At the Bibliotheque Nationale in Paris, it's called "L'enfer" or "Hell" collection. The British Museum calls it the "Arcana" collection, from the Latin word for mystery. At the Armed Forces Medical Library in Washington, where such squeamishness would be least expected, erotica is stashed in the "Cherry Case." At Harvard, it's kept in the "Hell Hole," and the Library of Congress preserves much of its erotic material in the "Delta" collection, from the Greek symbol for the female sex organ. The Brooklyn Public Library keeps its erotica in the main branch's "Treasure Room," while at the New York Public Library it's sequestered in "The Cage," a fenced off portion of the stacks whose key is entrusted only to more senescent members of the staff.

Of course, among libraries, as among American girls visiting Paris, there will always be the one or two exceptions who are more forthright in acknowledging their sexual resources. In this respect, the collection of erotica in the Vatican Library is probably most accessible to the non-professional bibliophile. L'enfer collection at the Bibliotheque Nationale in Paris is next most accessible, a catalogue of its most distinguished works having been issued complete with library call numbers. The Library of Congress in Washington, commendably, is America's most liberal library in this respect. It will issue an erotic work to anyone over sixteen years of age, though an armed guard will be assigned to stand over the reader's shoulder, ready to shoot if the book is mutilated.

The Union Catalogue of the Library of Congress, incidentally, which lists the resources of every important library in the nation, can be put to valuable use by any reasonably knowledgeable bookman in confirming the existence of almost any important erotic work at any major library in the United States.

A researcher needs merely to look up the card of an erotic work either by its title or author and the whereabouts of the book at major libraries all across the country will be revealed by the Union catalogue.

PART VII *The Erotic Book Market Today*

IF ALL THIS has made the locating of classical erotica at libraries seem difficult, then the task of finding it in retail trade will appear well nigh impossible. Because of laws against the sale of erotica, the very few dealers who handle it do so with great temerity, and the prices are altitudinous. A decent copy of *Fanny Hill,* for example, (decent refers to the book's physical, not moral, condition) will move at $25, while an unexpurgated *Lady Chatterley's Lover* will fetch anywhere from $50 to $100. A copy of *One Hundred Merrie and Delightsome Stories,* a collection of scintillating off-color medieval tales, is worth $200 in good condition, while a set of Fuchs' *Sittengeschichte* generally brings $400 or more.

The ticker-tape of market prices on classical erotica is generally considered to be *American Book-Prices Current.* It is a periodical which records all transactions at the nation's leading book auctions, where much of America's classical erotica is traded. These auctions are almost all located in New York, the wholesale center for most of America's other implements of scholarship. Catalogues are issued by these auction galleries and erotica can generally be found under such veiled headings as "Amatory," "Curiosa," "Deliciae," "Esoteric," "Facetiae," "Occult," and "Varia."

A list of the erotic best-sellers as handled by these auctions and by other New York dealers would probably look something like this:

Fanny Hill (John Cleland)

Grushenka: Three Times a Woman (Anonymous)

Justine and Juliette, by the Marquis de Sade

The unexpurgated *Lady Chatterley's Lover* (D. H. Lawrence)

My Life and Loves (Frank Harris)

The Lustful Turk (Anonymous)

A Night in a Moorish Harem (Ascribed to Lord George Herbert)

The Perfumed Garden (Sheik Nefzaui)

Rosy Crucifixion, Sexus, Plexus, Tropic of Cancer, and *Tropic of Capricorn,* all by Henry Miller

Venus in Furs (Sacher-Masoch)

Only a Boy (Generally ascribed to Eugene Field)

There are signs that a wider and more literate American public is beginning to recognize the real artistic merit of some of these erotic works. The police and so-called vice-suppressing agencies, for example, have never yet raided the auction galleries where the more worthwhile specimens of erotic literature are traded. And even the august *New York Times* is beginning to accept "Books Wanted" classified ads for such works as Henry Miller's *Tropic of Capricorn* and *Tropic of Cancer.*

Still, the volume of trading in classical erotica in New York—and hence in the nation—remains a mere trickle, perhaps 25,000 volumes a year.

Far more important than New York as a center of English erotica, however, is Paris. It easily outstrips (if you'll pardon the use of the word) Brussels which was the world capital of bawdry until the end of World War II. The French capital now keeps at least three publishers of English erotica busy full time. Their annual output totals 200,000 volumes, almost half of which is said to reach the United States. The names of these three publishers are the Obelisk, Vendome and Olympia Presses.

They print not only unexpurgated translations of erotic classics like the Marquis de Sade's *Justine* and *Juliette,* but also standards like the works of Henry Miller. Occasionally they will also gamble on avante-guarde productions like *The Debauched Hospodar,* by Guillaume Apollinaire, the bombastic French poet who claimed credit for the "discovery" of Picasso. Fortunately for Olympia Press, the publisher of *The Debauched Hospodar,* this work has turned out to be the biggest seller on the Paris erotic book market today. Apollinaire penned the opus—regarded as a book without peer for extravagance of lubricity—in a contest with two other barroom literary lights to see who could turn out the most wanton novel.

Ironically, the Paris branch of Brentano's one of America's best loved bookstore chains, is said to carry *The Debauched Hospodar,* or works like it, because it is legal to do so in Paris.

As any author who's ever seen the photographs of Anita Ekberg in the men's magazines or tried to sell an honest play on sex to television well knows, this whole question of morality in the arts is easily one of the most bemuddled areas of conviction maintained by mankind.

Anthony Comstock, for example, the famous American vice-suppressor, once said that erotic literature was "a moral vulture which steals upon our youth, silently striking its terrible talons into their vitals, and forcibly bearing them away on hideous wings to shame and death." And an Elmhurst, New York, district attorney championed the same argument recently in a speech at an Elks' clubhouse when he stated that the country's shortage of teachers, engineers and scientists was attributable to the curse of erotic literature. Congressman Alfred D. Sieminski, of New Jersey, has even gone so far as to describe the presence of erotica in the United States as the handiwork of "an overall Communist plot."

Not all Americans, however, are quite so impressed or alarmed by the powers of erotica. Men like Arnold Bruce Levy, a young New York book dealer, stand on the other side of the argument. Says Mr. Levy:

"Most of the moralists in this country today feel that unless sex is made dull there will be entirely too much of it. This, of course, is absurd. Men and women have their capacities and it is my belief that they have operated at full throttle. So-called morality has never been a significant restrainer of sexual intercourse, just as erotica—despite the insinuations of certain book jacket blurbs—has never been an effective aphrodisiac. On the contrary, pornography and erotica are a release for pent up sexual frustration, not a promoter of it. No single crime has ever been conclusively traced to erotica, and I know of at least two psychiatrists who consider it valuable educational material for late adolescents in view of the almost universal lack of sex education in schools. Furthermore, I don't think I'll ever be able to understand why murder in literature is considered less immoral than fornication."

Dr. Benjamin Karpman, Chief Psychotherapist

at St. Elizabeth's Hospital in Washington, D. C., substantiates Levy's contentions. Writing in the *Journal of the American Medical Association,* he says:

"Contrary to popular misconception, people who read salacious literature are less likely to become sexual offenders than those who do not, for the reason that such reading often neutralizes what aberrant sexual interests they may have."

The late Theodore Schroeder, a brilliant civil liberties attorney and history's most dedicated student of the law of obscene literature, says of pornographic works:

"Truly we all have some emotional aversion to them, and the great mob with its crude thinking and its careless expression and ignorance asserts substantially that emotional disapproval and social danger are synonymous.

"We have all seen the bawdy pictures, and yet none of us was injured by the sight. No one ever knew of any other healthy person who was injured by viewing them. Yet so persistent has been the reiteration of injury, baseless except in our dreaded emotion, that every one *assumes* that they must be dangerous.

"Once open the door to a full and frank discussion of sex, and by thus satisfying the healthy and natural curiosity, soon the morbid curiosity will disappear. No one caricatures or is morbid about the sexual mechanism of our domestic animals only because we have no curiosity concerning them. When we get as healthy minded an attitude about human sexuality by satisfying and accurate information easily obtainable for all, then there will be no demand for such stuff as we now dread."

Most bookmen, it is safe to say, stand on the same side as Mr. Levy, Dr. Karpman and Mr. Schroeder. Every nation gets the pornography it deserves, they say again and again, and if we forbid the writing of erotica to all but those willing to break the law, we have no complaint if the results are mean and inartistic. In this connection, Alec Craig, in his brilliant review of anti-obscenity law, *Above All Liberties,* offers a ray of hope for the future:

"Our society allows any amount of sexual stimulation at all times by poster, newspaper, cinema, theatre and women's dress in public; but it frowns on sexual satisfaction and aids thereto. In the society of the future (if indeed men are advancing to a better world) I believe that this emphasis will be reversed. Life will be less sex-obsessed but, at proper times and seasons, physical love will be restored to its ancient dignity, variety and gaiety. Both modesty and the art of love will come into their own again. In that society the erotic book, we may expect, will play a part."

Bibliography of One Hundred Titles

1. ADULTERY ON THE PART OF MARRIED WOMEN AND FORNICATION ON THE PART OF OLD MAIDS AND WIDOWS, DEFENDED BY MARY WILSON, SPINSTER, WITH PLANS FOR PROMOTING SAME.

2. ADVENTURES OF A KING'S PAGE. Published by Charles White, London, 1829.

3. THE AMATORY ADVENTURES OF A SURGEON WHO AVAILED HIMSELF OF HIS CONFIDENTIAL POSITION TO TAKE ADVANTAGE OF THE INNOCENCE OF PRURIENCY OF HIS PATIENTS.

4. AMELIA MORTON; OR LIFE AT A FASHIONABLE WATERING PLACE. Anon.

5. AMOROUS PASSION AT DIFFERENT STAGES IN LIFE, by La Popeliniere.

6. ANECDOTA AMERICANA. Anon.

7. ANTHROPOLOGICAL STUDIES IN THE STRANGE SEXUAL PRACTICES OF ALL RACES IN ALL AGES, ANCIENT AND MODERN, by Dr. Iwan Bloch. Translated from the German. Limited Edition. Anthropological Press, New York, 1933.

8. THE BAR MAID OF OLD POINT HOUSE, BEING THE SECRET HISTORY OF THE AMOURS AND INTRIGUES OF A BAR MAID WHOSE AMOROUS DISPOSITION AND VOLUPTUOUS ACHIEVEMENTS ON THE COUCH OF CUPID MADE HER THE ENVY OF HER OWN SEX AND THE ADMIRATION OF THE NEW WORLD.

9. THE BATTLE OF VENUS; A DESCRIPTIVE DISSERTATION ON THE VARIOUS MODES OF ENJOYMENT. Translated from the posthumous works of Voltaire. (Not authentic). London, 1760.

10. BEDSTEAD, THE CURIOUS AND DIVERTING HISTORY AND ADVENTURES OF A BEDSTEAD, CONTAINING MANY SINGULAR AND INTERESTING AMOROUS TALES AND NARRATIVES: PEEP INTO THE SERAGLIO: FORMING ONE OF THE MOST MOVING HISTORIES EVER DISPLAYED TO THE PUBLIC OF AMOURS IN HIGH AND LOW LIFE, EMBELLISHED WITH APPROPRIATE PLATES, London, 1840.

11. BIBLIOTHECA CURIOSA ET EROTICA, by Bernhard Stern-Szana, 1921.

12. THE BRIDE'S CONFESSION IN A LETTER TO HER FRIEND BELLA, otherwise entitled THE BRIDAL NIGHT, a poem attributed to Lord Byron. Paris, 1917.

13. THE CABINET OF VENUS, including THE FARMER'S DAUGHTER, BOUND FOR INDIA ON THE P & O STEAMER, CHINESE CHARADES, AND CONFESSIONS OF A VIRTUOUS WIFE. Illustrated. Erotica Bibliomaniac Society, London, 1896.

14. CATENA LIBRORUM TACENDORUM, by Henry Spencer Ashbee.

15. A CLASSICAL DICTIONARY OF THE VULGAR TONGUE, by Captain Grose.

16. THE CONFESSIONS OF MARIE ANTOINETTE.

17. CONFESSIONS OF A VOLUPTUOUS YOUNG LADY OF HIGH RANK, DISCUSSING HER SECRET LONGINGS AND PRIVATE AMOURS BEFORE FORMING A CURIOUS PICTURE OF REFINED SENSUALITY. London, Printed for the Society of Vice, 1860.

18. CONVERSATION AT THE SOCIAL FIRESIDE AS IT WAS IN YE TIME OF YE TUDORS. Temp. Circ. 1601. Mark Twain.

19. CRIPP'S MONTHLY, a monthly, issued in New York, 1876-7. Complete issue said to be unknown.

20. THE CUPID. 1891.

21. CURIOSITIES OF FLAGELLATION: A SERIES OF INCIDENTS AND FACTS COLLECTED BY AN AMATEUR FLAGELLANT. London, 1875.

22. A DIALOGUE OF STAYS, by Major Edward Markham (pseud).

23. THE DIARY OF A NYMPHOMANIAC.

24. DICTIONAIRE EROTIQUE, by Delvau.

25. DOCTOR'S POCKET COMPANION AND MARRIAGE GUIDE, by James Teller. Albany, New York, 1864.

26. L'ENFER DE LA BIBLIOTHEQUE NATIONALE, by Perceau.

27. DAS EROTISCHE ELEMENT IN DER KARIKATUR, by Eduard Fuchs. Berlin, 1904.

28. EROTISMO E PORNOGRAFIA NEL ROMANZO FRANCESE MODERNO, by Domenico Fusco. Torino, 1948.

29. EXPERIENCES OF FLAGELLATION; Instances of Whipping inflicted on Both Sexes; With Curious Anecdotes of Ladies. Compiled by an Amateur Flagellant. London, 1885.

30. THE FESTIVAL OF LOVE, a collection of 150 ribald and titillating poems.

31. FLORA MONTGOMERY, THE FACTORY GIRL; A tale of the Lowell factories, being a recital of the adventures of a libidinous millionaire whose wealth was used as a means of triumphing over virtue, by Sparks. New York, 1856, George Atkinson and Co.

32. FLOSSIE. Anon.
33. GAMIANI, by De Musset.
34. GESCHICHTE DER EROTIK, by Carl Van Bolen, 1951.
35. GLOSSARIUM EROTICUM, by Pierre Pierrugues, 1826.
36. THE GOLDEN LOTUS, translation from the Chinese novel, CHIN P'ING MEI. Four volumes. New York, 1954.
37. GRUSHENKA: THREE TIMES A WOMAN. Anon.
38. MISS HIGH HEELS. The story of a rich but young man under the control of his pretty step sister and her aunt, written by him at this step sister's order, with an account of his punishments, the dresses he was made to wear, his final subjection and his curious fate. Privately printed in Paris, 1931.
39. HISTORIA AMORIS, A History of Love, Ancient and Modern, by Saltus (pseud.). New York, 1906.
40. HISTORY OF FLAGELLATION AMONG DIFFERENT NATIONS. A Narrative of Strange Customs and Cruelties of the Romans, Greeks and Egyptians, with an account of its practice as a religious stimulant and corrector of Morals. Also Cases of remarkable Floggings and of celebrated Flagellants. London, 1888.
41. THE HORN BOOK. Anon.
42. HOW TO RAISE LOVE, OR THE ART OF MAKING LOVE IN MORE WAYS THAN ONE. London, 1828.
43. ILLUSTRIERTE SITTENGESCHICHTE, by Eduard Fuchs. Published by Albert Langen, Munchen, 1909.
44. INDEX LIBRORUM PROHIBITORUM, by Henry Spencer Ashbee, London, 1877.
45. JOHN, THE DARLING OF THE PHILADELPHIA LADIES. Anon.
46. JOSEPHINE MUTZENBACHER. Anon.
47. THE KAMA SUTRA, by Vatsya Yana.

48. LADY CHATTERLEY'S LOVER, by D. H. Lawrence. 1928.

49. LETTERS FROM LAURA AND EVELINE: GIVING AN ACCOUNT OF THEIR MOCK MARRIAGE, WEDDING TRIP, ETC. Eight volumes, privately printed, London, 1883.

50. LITERATUR UND KUNST, Bilder-Lexicon.

51. A LUSCIOUS TALE OF A SUCCESSFUL PHYSIOLOGICAL SEARCH AFTER REJUVENESCENCE, FULLY DISCLOSING THE SECRET OF THE ONLY NATURAL AND TRUE ELIXIR CAPABLE OF EFFECTING SUCH A DESIRABLE NECESSITY, by David II (pseud). Jerusalem, 1851.

52. THE LUSTFUL TURK, with beautiful engravings, by an Arcadian. 1828.

53. MEMOIRS AND ADVENTURES OF A FLEA. London, 1785.

54. THE MEMOIRS OF DOLLY MORTON. Society of Private Bibliophiles, Philadelphia, 1904.

55. MEMOIRS OF A MAN OF PLEASURE. Anon.

56. MEMOIRS OF A RUSSIAN PRINCESS. Anon.

57. MEMOIRS OF A WOMAN OF PLEASURE, by John Cleland. London.

58. THE MERRY MUSES OF CALEDONIA: A COLLECTION OF FAVOURITE SCOT SONGS, compiled by Robert Burns.

59. THE MERRY ORDER OF ST. BRIDGET: PERSONAL RECOLLECTIONS OF THE USE OF THE ROD.

60. MISSBRAUCH DER WISSENSCHAFT IN DER LITERATUR UBER EROTIK, by M. Kesselring.

61. MY LIFE AND LOVES, by Frank Harris.

62. MY SECRET LIFE. London, 1888.

63. A NIGHT IN A MOORISH HAREM, by Lord George Herbert. Erotica Biblion Society of London and New York.

64. THE NIGHT SCHOOL, by Major Edward Markham (pseud).

65. THE OLD MAN YOUNG AGAIN, OR AGE REJUVENESCENCE IN THE POWER OF CONCUPISCENCE. Literally translated from the Arabic by an English Bohemian. Excurses on the Uses of Aphrodisiacs. The author has written the book for the purpose of exciting to connection those who are indifferent thereto. Privately printed on Dutch handmade paper, Aden, MDCCCXCVIII.

66. ONE HUNDRED MERRIE AND DELIGHTSOME STORIES, Right Pleasaunt to Relate in All Goodly Companie, originally titled LES CENT NOUVELLES NOUVELLES, Translated by Robert B. Douglas. Charles Carrington, publisher, Paris, 1899.

67. 120 JOURNEES DE SODOME, by the Marquis de Sade.

68. THE OXFORD PROFESSOR. Anon.

69. PAULINE, THE PRIMA DONNA, OR MEMOIRS OF AN OPERA SINGER. London and New York, 1898.

70. THE PERFUMED GARDEN, by the Sheikh Nefzaui. Fortune Press, London, 1934.

71. PLEXUS, by Henry Miller.

72. THE PROGRESS OF SEDUCTION OF A HIGHLY EDUCATED YOUNG LADY WHO BECAME THE VICTIM OF DEBAUCHERY AND LIBERTINISM. New York, 1854, H.S.G. Smith and Company.

73. RATI-SASTRAM, Or The Greatest Work on Hindu System of Sexual Science. Translated from Sanscrit. Calcutta, 1908.

74. REGISTRUM LIBRORUM EROTICORUM, compiled by Rolf S. Reade (Pseud. for Alfred Rose). London, 1936.

75. THE ROMANCE OF CHASTISEMENT, by Major Edward Markham (pseud).

76. SCATALOGIC RITES OF ALL NATIONS, A dissertation upon the employment of excrementitious remedial agents in religion, therapeutics, divination, witchcraft, love-philtres, etc., in all parts of the globe, by Capt. John G. Bourke, Third Cavalry, USA. Lowdermilk and Co., Washington, 1891.

77. THE SECRET SERVICES AND DUTIES OF MAJOR LOVITT, BEING A NOVEL OF THE CIVIL WAR.

78. SEXUAL LIFE IN ENGLAND, by Iwan Bloch. London, 1938.

79. SEXUS, by Henry Miller.

80. SODOM, by John Wilmot, the Earl of Rochester.

81. SODOM IN UNION SQUARE, OR REVELATIONS OF THE DOINGS IN FOURTEENTH STREET, by An Ex-Police Captain of New York.

82. SOME LIMERICKS, by Norman Douglas. Collected for the use of students. Privately printed in Florence, 1928.

83. SPORTSMAN'S SLANG, by John Bee.

84. THE STORY OF A DILDOE; A TALE IN FIVE TABLEAUX. London, 1880.

85. TEN YEARS OF THE LIFE OF A COURTESAN—DETAILING HER LESSONS IN LUST, HER SEDUCTION AND VOLUPTUOUS LIFE, THE PIQUANT PENCHANTS OF HER VARIOUS LOVERS. Illustrated.

86. THESAURUS EROTICUS LINGUAE LATINAE, Stuttgart, 1883.

87. THE THIRTY-SIX JOYS OF A WOMAN.

88. TITANEN EROTIK, by Eduard Fuchs.

89. THE TOAST, by Dr. William King.

90. TROPIC OF CANCER, by Henry Miller.

91. TROPIC OF CAPRICORN, by Henry Miller.

92. THE UPS AND DOWNS OF LIFE. By one who has been behind the scene and taken part in performance. Printed in Ireland, 1879.

93. USEFUL HINTS TO SINGLE GENTLEMEN RESPECTING MARRIAGE, CONCUBINAGE, AND ADULTERY. In prose and verse. By J. Cruikshanks. London, 1792. Contains The Artful Seducer, The Melancholy Consequences of a Seduction, and A Dying Harlot's Address to an old Debauchee.

94. THE VOLUPTUARIAN CABINET, BEING A DIALOGUE BETWEEN A MAID AND A WHORE.

95. THE WAY TO PEEL, by Major Edward Markham (pseud).

96. THE WEDDING NIGHT; Being the Interesting Life of a Courtesan of Quality Compelled by Necessity to Prostitute her Person for Gold, Becoming Famous for her Artful and Licentious Methods of Raising the Animal Spirits, of Reviving the Drooping Energy of Age and of Restoring to the Expiring Torch a New Light, the Whole Being a Most Interesting Narrative of Intrigue and Debauchery. Illustrated with Curious Engravings. By John Duncombe, J. Turner & Co., Holywell Street, London, 1830.

97. WHOREDOM. THE MYSTERIES OF WHOREDOM, REVEALED IN A CORRESPONDENCE BETWEEN MISS LOVEMAN AND MISS LONGFORT, TWO BLOOMING CYPRIANS IN FULL TRADE, INTERSPERSED WITH NUMEROUS INTERESTING ANECDOTES, DIVERS INTERESTING STORIES, SUNDRY DROLL ADVENTURES, A VARIETY OF COMIC INCIDENTS, AND AN EXTENSIVE FUND OF VOLUPTUOUS RECREATIONS AND INCITEMENT. Embellished with beautiful cuts. Printed for the Society of Vice. Dugdale, printers. London, 1860.

98. THE WHORE'S RHETORICK.

99. THE WOMAN OF HONOR, by John Cleland, London, 1768.

100. WORSHIP OF PRIAPUS; Influence of the Phallic Idea in the Religions of Antiquity, by Hodder M. Westropp and C. Staniland Wake. J. W. Bouton, New York, 1874.

Index